HIDDEN HEADLINES

AN UNINTENTIONAL MEMOIR

MAL WALDEN

Published by Brolga Publishing Pty Ltd
ABN 46 063 962 443
PO Box 452
Torquay Victoria 3228
Australia
email: markzocchi@brolgapublishing.com.au

All rights reserved. No part of this publication may be reproduced, stored in a retrieval system or transmitted in any form or by any means electronic, mechanical, photocopying, recording or otherwise without prior permission from the publisher.

Copyright © 2025 Mal Walden

National Library of Australia
Cataloguing-in-Publication data

ISBN: 978-1-7640776-1-3 (paperback)

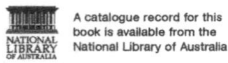
A catalogue record for this book is available from the National Library of Australia

Printed in Australia
Cover design and typeset by WorkingType Studio

BE PUBLISHED
Publish through a successful publisher.
National Distribution to Australia & New Zealand
International Distribution to the United Kingdom
Ebooks Worldwide Sales Representation to South East Asia

PREFACE

"Hidden Headlines" is a captivating collection of extraordinary personal stories, intimate confessions, and inspirational encounters. It's an unplanned memoir exploring untold narratives from behind some of our major headline news. It's a selection of stories by those who may not have made the news but unknowingly shaped the news – one headline at a time. Their stories are as diverse as they are compelling, offering fresh perspectives on well-known events or unveiling secrets that have remained hidden until now.

They may not all be sensational stories. There are dreams, friendships, hope, survival and often tragedy.

Having spent a lifetime in the media, I have discovered everyone has a story to tell if you are prepared to listen, so perhaps now is the time to share some of their memories.

I begin with a very personal story that continues to haunt those of us connected with the 1975 East Timor massacre in a once-insignificant village called Balibo.

CONTENTS

Balibo, 50 years.   7
From one of Australia's darkest chapters comes deeply felt tributes in memory of five murdered journalists.

Valkyrie.   21
A Melbourne woman shares a deeply personal experience of her uncle's attempt to assassinate Adolf Hitler.

The Tattoo.   32
A life changed forever as an air traffic controller, tracks her pilot husband as his plane crashes into the World Trade Centre.

Princess Diana.   41
A personal conversation and an unexpected royal confession.

Miracle at the Crease.   51
A young cricketer's miraculous survival from the Boxing Day Tsunami.

Contents

Just a boy from 'Sandy'.   60
Tributes to a local lad who shaped Australian Television.

Munich Olympic Massacre.   74
Two Australians emerged from the Olympic tragedy—one became a TV legend, the other a Prime Minister.

Alive in the Andes.   89
A personal account of modern history's most harrowing and inspiring tale of cannibalism and survival.

Ugandan Leader Idi Amin.   100
A Melbourne colleague reveals how he created a worldwide myth that continues to this day.

Lethal Legacy.   108
A dying colleague reveals hush money and corporate coverups as asbestos cancer strikes media workers.

Tunnel Vision.   120
There's an unwritten rule in television – no pictures, no story. After a near tragedy in Melbourne's hidden tunnels, I was left with words only.

A Personal Curtain Call. 131

A stage-door start to a six-decade career in media, beginning at The Firm with Australian Theatre legends, Sir Frank Tait and John MacCallum.

A Load of Old Crocs. 144

Crocodiles in the suburbs highlight the potential dangers of keeping exotic pets and the risks they pose to both the animals and the community.

The White Light. 155

"I've been to the other side and I can tell you there's nothing fucking there". Kerry Packer's blunt near-death experience contrasts with others' accounts of the afterlife.

My Hidden Headlines. 167

CHAPTER 1

Balibo 50 years

Top left: Malcolm Rennie, Greg Shackleton,
Bottom left: Gary Cunningham, Brian Peters, Tony Stewart.

The legacy of Balibo stands as a symbol of shame and unresolved heartache; a deeply personal story that continues to haunt those of us connected to that tragic event.

It's now 50 years since five Australian journalists, including three close colleagues, were brutally murdered by invading Indonesian troops in that once insignificant town in East Timor.

For 50 years, the story of Balibo has played out in cinemas, courts and headline news around the world. But behind the headlines lies a personal story; one that was built on acceptance, identity, hope and courage.

* * *

On Wednesday, 1 October 1975, the fate of three of my colleagues was sealed with a toss of a coin. The choice of who to send to cover the developing crisis in East Timor had been narrowed down to two, since others, including myself, had been eliminated.

Melbourne reporter Greg Shackleton had convinced our news boss, John Maher, that he had secured the appropriate contacts necessary to succeed.

Sydney's ATN7 reporter Brian Anderson, who at least

had some Vietnam experience, had similarly convinced his boss he was the most qualified.

John Maher and his Sydney-based counterpart Bob Johnston were operating news departments under a very complicated and at times highly volatile de facto Network relationship.

ATN7 was owned by Sydney's Fairfax, and HSV7 was owned by Melbourne's Herald and Weekly Times. In a bid to avoid another of their frequent fiery clashes, Bob Johnston offered a compromise with a simple toss of a 20-cent coin. Johnston elected to toss the coin in Sydney while Maher called "heads" in Melbourne. There was a pause as the coin was heard to make its final spin.

Then the voice of Johnston simply said, 'It's heads for Shackleton,' and hung up.

* * *

October 10, 1975, reporter Greg Shackleton, cameraman Gary Cunningham and assistant Tony Stewart arrived in the small village of Balibo in East Timor to document the presence of Indonesian warships amid growing fears of an imminent invasion. They were joined by Malcolm Rennie and Brian Peters from the Nine Network – to be remembered as the 'Balibo 5'.

Thursday evening, October 15, almost one week after they had left Melbourne, I was clearing my desk and preparing to leave the newsroom when my phone rang.

The voice I heard would be one of the most haunting calls I have ever received. 'My son is dead' 'My son is dead'. 'I know what has happened... It's a mother's intuition,' she kept repeating... 'I know it ... I feel it ... I know he's dead.'

I was about to ask who was speaking when she identified herself as Greg Shackleton's mother.

'My son is dead, he's been killed ... Oh my God! Please help!'

I began trying to console her, to convince her she was wrong, telling her if anything had happened, we would be among the first to know.

She was wrong.

Greg was very much alive when his mother rang me. He was killed along with four other Australian newsmen in the early hours of the following morning.

It wasn't a mother's intuition, as she kept repeating. It was a mother's terrible premonition.

The Balibo Five, as they are remembered, were murdered by Indonesian forces as they stormed the dusty little village of Balibo with no intention of taking prisoners. The fact that Greg Shackleton had painted the Australian flag on the building they were living in did nothing to save them.

* * *

John Milkins

John Milkins was just five years old when the Balibo Five were brutally killed during the Indonesian invasion of East Timor in 1975.

No one could have imagined how that tragic event would one day become so deeply personal to him.

At the age of 20, John's journey of discovery began with a decision to explore his heritage. Knowing he had been adopted as a baby and raised by loving parents who had always supported him, he says he felt a deep, inexplicable need to understand where he came from. "I had everything I needed," he reflected, "but there was this indescribable core drive that I felt I had to know where I had come from—to know where I was going."

His search finally led him to a government office, where he sat down to open a manila file to discover hidden details of his first life.

He described that moment in time as 'surreal'. Inside the file, he found the name "Edward Giles Norman," his birth name, along with the name of his mother, Heather Norman, who was just 21 years old at the time of his birth. The space for his father's name simply read: "unknown."

That was the start of his second journey. With the support of his adoptive parents, John began the search for his birth mother. Using electoral rolls and with the help of others, he eventually tracked down Heather Norman, who was living in Frankston. Heather agreed to meet John and that's where the missing pieces of his early life all began to fall into shape.

She told him that she was a 21-year-old student teacher when she met a TV cameraman while working on a documentary about the new Ned Kelly movie starring Mick Jagger. She described Gary as large, full of life who literally swept her off her feet.

Their connection, she said, was 'brief but significant'. After a short affair, Heather became pregnant and by the time she realised she was carrying a child, he had been posted elsewhere, and the two lost contact with each other.

Heather was then left to face the challenges of an unplanned pregnancy alone. For weeks, she agonised over what to do. She named her baby boy Edward because he reminded her of a teddy bear. But as a single mother in the 1970s, a time when support for unmarried mothers was virtually non-existent, Heather made the heart-wrenching decision to give him up for adoption. She believed that her six-week-old son would have a far better chance at life in a two-parent family. Edward was adopted by a caring couple who raised him as John Milkins.

It was during their initial meeting that Heather

revealed the identity of John's father, a detail that had been left blank on his birth certificate: 'Gary Cunningham', one of the Balibo Five.

The revelation stunned John. "That absolutely freaked me out as I had recently completed a study on the Balibo Five during an international relations class at university. The connection felt almost too extraordinary to believe".

The discovery opened a new chapter in John's life. Not only did he learn about his father, but he also found himself part of a larger family he never knew existed. "About two weeks after uncovering the truth, I met nearly eighty of Heather's family, all of whom had been unaware of my existence until then".

"It was an overwhelming but deeply meaningful experience as I began to piece together the missing parts of my identity".

He then contacted Gary's family, who initially voiced some doubt over the authenticity of his claims but slowly accepted John into their loving family.

John described the enormous enjoyment of seeing both families coming together as one, while maintaining the lasting love of his adoptive parents, who he still called 'Mum and Dad'.

"I have since learnt the most amazing things about my mother's family, including my uncle Peter Norman, who won Silver at the Mexico Olympics and is still remembered for his support for that controversial black power salute".

Then over a family lunch one day, another relative revealed he was the pilot who flew the Balibo Five from Darwin to Dili in 1975. "Just another sliding door moment in my life".

John says he then spent a 'fairly dark time' researching Gary's death through the library and microfilm footage, viewing horrible descriptions of what had happened that day in Balibo and trying to understand why our Government did so little to investigate their deaths and too ready to accept the Indonesian account they were caught in the crossfire.

He describes the evidence withheld in secrecy, evidence of Australia's prior knowledge of the massacre and subsequent invasion of East Timor, as overwhelming.

Thursday, 16 October 1975

Just before dawn on that fateful morning, the newsmen were awoken by the sounds of artillery, mortars and tank fire coming from the direction of the nearby town of Batugade. The attack consisted of three Special Forces teams supplemented by regular Indonesian Para Commandos and supported by heavy bombardment from seven warships, stationed off the coast.

It's believed both cameramen, Gary Cunningham from Seven and Brian Peters from Nine, had moved out and begun filming. While filming, eyewitnesses saw other crewmembers Shackleton, Rennie and Stewart emerge from the building shouting and gesturing to the advancing troops. They were calling out that they were Australians and pointing to the Australian flag that Greg had painted on the side of the house they had been living in. All five journalists were outside when the first soldiers began firing. Four immediately turned and ran towards the nearby Chinese house with their arms in the air, still yelling 'Australian... Australian!'

When the troops entered the square the four journalists who had made it safely to the house slowly emerged with their hands in the air, repeating the words "journalists" and "Australian". The journalist at the front was then seen to have been either stabbed, shot or both, depending on eyewitness accounts. The others were herded back into the house and machine-gunned. However, it's believed one of them survived by hiding in a bathroom at the rear of the house and was subsequently executed.

Eyewitnesses say the attack lasted just over 45 minutes. By 7 a.m. local time, it was all over. The bodies, including an injured newsman who had fled up the hill where he died, were then gathered up. There are slightly differing versions of the events that followed. One has the Indonesians pouring liquid over the bodies and setting them on fire.

Whatever the truth, by early evening, the five journalists were lying burnt beyond recognition in a Chinese house across the street from the house where they pitifully daubed the flag and the word "Australia" in the hope it would afford them some protection.

For John Milkins, it was not just the deaths of five Australians, six with Roger East, but over 183,000 Timorese that followed the invasion. "I couldn't understand as a young man, becoming an angry young man, how this horrific tragedy had occurred on our doorstep, and our country seemed to be deliberately burying the truth.

In 2002, the Victorian government of Steve Bracks set up the Balibo House Trust and invited family members, including John Milkins, to join. Together with Channel 7, 9, Multiplex World Vision, and many other generous sponsors, they refurbished the Balibo flag house in East Timor, where Greg Shackleton had painted the Australian flag on the wall and turned it into a working community centre. It was the first time in 25 years that a government had acknowledged the Balibo tragedy. And it took a State government to do it.

16 November 2007, NSW Magistrate Dorelle Pinch released her findings from a lengthy inquest into the deaths of Brian Peters and the Balibo five. She found they died from wounds sustained after being shot or stabbed and were not killed in the heat of battle or crossfire as accepted by the Australian Government. The purpose of the report she said "was to demonstrate that the truth is never too young to be told, nor too old'. She then stepped outside of her mandate and referred the case to the AFP and the Attorney General's Department as a possible war crime.

October 2014, the case was dropped. Australian Federal Police abandoned the war-crime investigation on the grounds of 'insufficient evidence to prove an offence'.

Crucially, there are no statutes of limitations for war

crimes, meaning those responsible can still be held accountable, no matter how much time has passed.

October 2025.

As surviving family and friends attended the 50th Anniversary of that fateful day, it was also an occasion to celebrate the achievements of the Balibo House Trust, established in memory of the murdered journalists.

Since its opening in 2003, it has proudly achieved significant community development in the Balibo district of Timor-Leste.

Partnered by Rotary and other sponsors, the Trust has established the Balibo Five Kindergarten while supporting five primary schools in the surrounding areas.

They have established the Balibo Community Learning Centre, offering training skills in areas of motor mechanics, carpentry, sewing and hospitality.

The Balibo Dental Clinic provides free dental care and education, staffed by Timorese with Australian volunteer support. While the Balibo Fort Hotel and Museum has boosted tourism and employment.

All these efforts by the trust have enhanced health education and economic opportunities while preserving the memory of the Balibo Five.

Meanwhile, the campaign for truth surrounding the massacre, the invasion, the brutality that followed and alleged Australian complicity continues quietly but persistently to this day.

Thanks to John Milkins of the Balibo House Trust, Melbourne Age, ABC's Australian Story, and Melbourne Press Club's Freedom Dinner, September 2015.

CHAPTER 2

Valkyrie Vendetta

Around every corner, on every seat in any bus or train, are people with stories to tell.

Some of the best stories come from Melbourne's migrants, whose stories are so life-changing, that when retold, can reshape our own. All it takes is a moment in time for someone to listen. As I did on a Saturday night during a noisy South Yarra dinner party and heard first-hand a story that would inspire this book.

October 2008, South Yarra

By mid-evening the party was in full swing and the noise level had increased to a point that made conversation difficult. I began to empathise with an elderly guest, sitting on a couch sipping her rose-coloured champagne with a fixed smile and an occasional nod of recognition to other guests but otherwise rendered mute by the peripheral sound around her. She appeared to be in her 80s.

I wandered over, sat down next to her and introduced myself. Her first words spoke volumes.

"Hello, my name is Eve, so tell me Mal, how did you spend your day today?" Her blue eyes sparkled with intelligence and humour. She spoke with a strong European accent clipped by a recent stroke yet softened by the past twenty years or more of living in Melbourne. I had to concentrate to hear her above the noise from the room but with no idea of what I was about to hear.

In reply to her opening question, I told her I had spent

the afternoon at the movies with my wife. It was then her demeanour perceptibly changed. "I refuse to go to the movies since my row with that silly little film man ."

Slightly bemused, I asked who the 'silly little film-man' might be? "Tom Cruise," she replied without a moment of hesitation. "THE Tom Cruise?"

"Yes, he has made a film about my family and we are not very happy." "May I ask why Tom Cruise would make a film about your family?"

"It was my uncle, Claus Von Stauffenberg, who put the bomb under Adolph Hitler."

Everyone has a story to tell if you are prepared to listen and Eve now had my full attention. I was fully aware that the film *Valkyrie* was in post-production.

For the next 30 minutes, I sat spellbound as this sprightly 87-year-old with a slightly aristocratic air, recounted her uncle's failed attempt to assassinate one of the world's most despotic dictators. And as I sat next to the niece of the 'would-be assassin' the horror of Hitler's retribution was clearly showing on her face 64 years later.

What she failed to tell me during our initial encounter was the rest of her amazing life story: a life that included a brief spell as an award-winning

European film starlet – before the war – alongside such iconic names as Marlene Dietrich and Ilse Werner; her amazing survival from Hitler's henchmen and an incredible escape from invading Russians; becoming an interpreter to Field Marshal Montgomery in post-war Germany; and finally, a love story that led to her starting a new life here in Melbourne.

Eve's long-term memory was astounding as she relived details from the night of the Hitler assassination attempt.

Eve said she was around 21 at the time her Uncle Claus carried the briefcase bomb into the wooden barrack of the German high command in what was code-named 'Operation Valkyrie'.

She described the Stauffenberg family as one of the oldest most distinguished Roman Catholic families in southern Germany and revealed how she was related on her father's side through marriage. Claus Philip von Stauffenberg was the third of three sons, well-educated and inclined towards literature, but eventually took up a military career joining his family's traditional regiment.

However, from the outbreak of war in 1939 he became increasingly concerned at the criminal nature of Hitler's regime. A view, Eve said she was unaware of, but a growing view shared by others, including select members of her own family.

By 1944 Stauffenberg had risen to the rank of colonel and was one of few who had direct access to the Fuehrer.

"I met Hitler on the several occasions he visited our family," recounted Eve, "but we were young and unaware that Uncle Claus saw no other alternative for the future of Germany than in his assassination."

On 20 July that year, Uncle Claus carried his briefcase containing two small bombs, only one of which would be activated. He slid the case under the conference table, as close to Hitler as he could and made an excuse to leave.

He waited in a nearby shelter as the blast ripped through the building, killing four people and injuring many others, including his intended target, who was shielded from the full blast by the heavy oak table.

Hitler's retribution was as swift as it was violent.

Recounting this event 64 years later, Eve visibly stiffened at the horror that followed. "He ordered the execution of all the male members of my family." It began with a hastily convened impromptu court-marshal that condemned the ringleaders to death.

Claus Stauffenberg and his fellow officers were immediately arrested, many taken out and shot by a makeshift firing squad in the glare of vehicle headlights. According to Eve,"...others were slowly garrotted by piano wire."

At this stage of her story, Eve straightened her dress, stood and excused herself as she left the room.

Despite many attempts since that initial meeting in 2008 Eve refused all requests for a further interview. It would take me another nine years before the rest of her amazing life story fell into place. According to her daughter, Eve was a very pragmatic woman. "She would say, 'What's done is done. Forget the past and look to the future."

I was more interested in her past; the irony of her history as a European film star in the 30s and her issue with Tom Cruise.

Upon further investigation, I discovered a strong authoritative influence from her family in Germany, particularly Berthold von Stauffenberg, the eldest son of Claus's five children, who was 10 years old at the time of the assassination attempt.

While Operation Valkyrie had already been well documented at the time I met Eve, the family in

Germany had lodged strong objections to the choice of Tom Cruise in the lead role for this latest film.

According to 72-year-old Berthold, "It's unpleasant for me, that an avowed Scientologist will be playing my father."

However, Stauffenberg's grandson, 41-year-old Casper Graf von Stauffenberg didn't appear to have any fundamental problem with it. "After all, it's (film) a good medium for explaining history," he claimed.

The film came and went without breaking any box office records, but I doubt Eve ever saw it.

The day after the assassination attempt, Eve recalled the family hearing a radio broadcast denouncing a 'criminal attack' on Hitler but remembered any questions by the children were quickly evaded.

On 22 July, Countess Nina told her two eldest sons that it was their father who had carried out the attack on Hitler. The boys were thunderstruck and would later claim, "Our world broke apart in an instant." In all, some say up to 5000 were condemned in mock trials and many including Stauffenberg were executed.

On 16 August, 1944, nearly a month after the assassination attempt, the Stauffenberg children were taken to a Catholic priest for his blessing. He told them that it was likely that bad times awaited but 'they must never forget what their Claus had died for'.

The next day they were transported by train to a children's home where they were separated according to age and gender, and joined by the children of other conspirators. They were unaware that plans were afoot to rename them since Hitler had decreed that the very name Stauffenberg should be wiped out.

Initially, they were to be sent to Buchenwald concentration camp; a fate they avoided thanks to the near-miraculous intervention of an Allied bombing raid.

The war was nearing its end by then and the party's authority was breaking down. The Nazis had no option but to drive the children back to their home and a few days later, on 12 April, the American army liberated them ahead of the advancing Russians.

Eve was also one of the lucky survivors but the war would leave its pain.

In 1942 her brother Fritz, a Stuka pilot in the Luftwaffe, was shot down in France but survived only to be killed 18 months later in the battle of Stalingrad. As the war entered its final stages, Eve's home was overrun by the advancing Russians who used the Schloss as their command post in what would become East Germany.

Somehow her mother singlehandedly faced the Russian troops while hiding her two daughters. However, Eve smuggled herself in a truckload of motorcycles and made it to the British-controlled city of Hanover. There according to family records, she used her charms and her school girl English to become an interpreter for Field Marshal Montgomery who was running the Allied Information Control Unit.

It was in Hanover that she met the dashing Scottish/Italian-born Hector Pelman and subsequently married conceiving a son Ashley before migrating to Melbourne in 1951.

The marriage soon ended and Eve met Stuart Esnouf an East Melbourne Doctor. Former husband Hector also remarried and so began a very amicable blended arrangement with both families that lasted a lifetime.

In 1966 travel regulations in Eastern Europe relaxed and Eve returned to be reunited with the few surviving members of her immediate family.

On returning to Melbourne Eve's life experiences had become almost legendary taking to the speaking circuit lecturing and describing life in East Germany and Russia where few travelled in the 60s and early 70s. Throughout the 70s and 80s, Eve was on the Lady

Mayoress committee heading many charity and fundraising events in Melbourne.

In later years, health became an issue which, according to her loving daughter Durelle 'her surgical interventions needed cataloguing. "No kidney stone, three strokes, diabetes, heart disease or the loss of an eye through melanoma, interfered with her life.

"Mum was a pack-a-day smoker until her tennis friends at Kooyong refused to share her room on overnight tournaments and only then did she give them up – not her friends, the cigarettes."

At 92 years of age, Eve became part of a successful world trial for an aortic heart valve, now a common procedure.

At the time of our conversation in the South Yarra apartment, Eve was still under the impression her father had been shot along with her Uncle Claus. It was only recently the family discovered Eve's father escaped execution only to die 18 months later in a Russian jail.

Ruth 'Eve' Esnouf (nee von Lieberenz) the niece of the man who attempted to blow up Adolph Hitler passed away in a Melbourne nursing home on 10 May 2017 just short of her 98th birthday.

Chapter 2 Valkyrie Vendetta

An extraordinary life of a Melbourne migrant and a testament to that observation – everyone has a story to tell if you are prepared to take the time to listen.

CHAPTER 3

Tattoo – Life 2

*'When asked what happened to Life 1
... came a story that changed all our lives'*

The tattoo was impossible to ignore. A delicate design in tasteful script around her wrist simply read, **Life 2.**

From the moment she was introduced to mutual friends, the tattoo seemed to radiate an unspoken story.

After the first introductions were made, no one at the table dared to ask. She had a quiet elegance, a softness

Chapter 3 Tattoo - Life 2

in her Boston accent that made everyone lean in a little closer when she spoke. There was something about her—a resilience, a strength tempered by an unseen sadness. But as the evening wore on, conversation began to flow as freely as the wine, and curiosity eventually got the better of one of the guests.

"What happened to **Life 1?**" he asked.

The question hung in the air, and the table collectively held its breath. She looked down at her wrist, running her thumb gently over the ink as if drawing strength from it. Then, with a small, sad smile, she began to answer.

"It was a beautiful Boston morning, clear blue skies with a gentle breeze. The kind of day that makes you think life couldn't be more perfect. I remembered feeling a little flutter of excitement as I got ready for work—my husband was piloting a flight that morning, and I knew I'd have a chance to track his plane on the radar. It always gave me a thrill to know he was up there, soaring through the skies while I guided him from below."

She paused, taking a sip of water. The group leaned forward, hanging on her every word.

"As an air traffic controller, I was working the early

shift. By the time I arrived at the centre, the usual rhythm of the day had already begun. I exchanged pleasantries with the night crew, poured myself a coffee, and settled into my station in front of the monitors. It was business as usual—until it wasn't."

"At 7.59, my husband was given final approval for take-off and Flight 11 began its nonstop service from Boston to Los Angeles".

Just before 8:14, he had climbed to 26,000 feet and was instructed to continue to his assigned cruising altitude of 35,000 feet.

From that moment all subsequent attempts to contact the flight suddenly failed to be acknowledged. The transponder, a device that communicates the plane's identity and altitude, appeared to have been turned off. Confusion rippled through the room as controllers tried to re-establish contact. The calm, methodical tone of their voices began to waver as they realised the plane was not responding.

At 8:19, a frantic phone call was received from a crew member: "The cockpit is not answering, somebody's stabbed in business class—and I think there's Mace—that we can't breathe—I don't know, I think we're getting hijacked."

Chapter 3 Tattoo – Life 2

Her voice faltered slightly. It seemed the restaurant had fallen silent. It hadn't really; it was just that the table was preparing for a horror about to be relived.

'You have to understand', she said, 'the air traffic control room is typically a hub of precision and order'.

This was about to be shattered by a series of unprecedented events that unfolded with terrifying speed. The controllers' screens showed the plane making an abrupt turn toward New York City.

The tension was palpable as they scrambled to alert military and law enforcement agencies.

At 8:23, a dispatcher tried unsuccessfully to contact the aircraft, triggering the first major alert.

At 8:25 Boston Centre received a communication from the hijacker who had pressed the wrong key and the message intended for the passengers was received by ground control. "Nobody moves". "Everything will be okay. If you try to make any moves, you'll endanger yourself and the aeroplane. Just stay quiet."

At 8:26, the plane was reported "flying erratically". A minute later, Flight 11 turned south. Another message from the crew member reported a man in first class had his throat slashed; two flight attendants had been stabbed as they attempted to contact the cockpit.

At 8:38 the plane began flying erratically again and was in a rapid descent.

It then began tracking south along the Hudson River. "I thought—hoped—that maybe the crew would be able to land at Newark Airport, that perhaps they were dealing with an emergency that hadn't entirely disabled the aircraft. But then..."

Her voice broke for the first time, and she pressed her fingers to her lips as if holding back the memory.

At 8:44 ground control asked the crew member to look out the window to determine where they were. "We are flying low. We are flying very, very low". Seconds later she said, "Oh my God we are way too low." The phone call ended.

At 8:46 am, the unthinkable happened. The controllers watched in stunned silence as Flight 11 disappeared from the radar as it struck the North Tower of the World Trade Centre.

The room erupted into a cacophony of screams, cries and disbelief while others desperately tried to coordinate with emergency services. The chaos intensified as news of the impact spread, and the reality of a terrorist attack began to sink in.

Before they could fully process the situation, a

Chapter 3 Tattoo – Life 2

second plane, United Airlines Flight 175, also stopped transmitting its transponder signal. The controllers watched in horror as it too changed course, heading directly for Manhattan. The room, once a model of efficiency, became a scene of frantic activity.

Just 17 minutes later, Flight 175 slammed into the South Tower. The controllers, already reeling from the first impact, were overwhelmed by the sheer scale of the catastrophe. The radar screens, now symbols of horror rather than safety, continued to track other planes in the airspace, each one a potential threat. The room was filled with a sense of helplessness as they realised they were witnessing a coordinated attack.

Amid the chaos, controllers worked tirelessly to ground all flights across the country, an unprecedented move that required immense focus and coordination. The stress was unbearable, with many struggling to maintain composure as they grappled with the magnitude of the tragedy.

The table was utterly still. No one dared to speak, no one dared to breathe until she continued her story.

"It wasn't until the chaos settled until the horror began to take shape, that I realised—it was his flight. My husband's flight. He was the pilot of Flight 11".

"I lost all reasonable concentration after that".

"It was unlike anything I'd ever experienced. The world was falling apart, and we were at the centre of it, trying to piece together what was happening in real-time".

Then the decision was made to shut down all New York airspace. Every plane had to land. Every single one.

She paused, looking around the table. "You have to understand, air traffic controllers are trained for emergencies. But this? This was something else entirely. It wasn't just one plane, or two—it was the whole system unravelling before our eyes. And in the middle of it all, I had to process the fact that my husband was gone."

She took another deep breath, her hand still resting on her wrist.

"We tracked more flights after that. United Airlines Flight 93, which eventually crashed in Pennsylvania, and American Airlines Flight 77, which hit the Pentagon. We didn't know at the time what was happening on board those planes, the heroism of the passengers who fought back. All we saw were the radar blips—the ones that disappeared, one by one."

She fell silent for a moment, her eyes distant, lost in

Chapter 3 Tattoo - Life 2

the memory. Then she looked back at the group, her voice softer now.

"September 11th didn't just end my husband's life. It ended mine, too—at least, the life I'd known. **Life 1** was gone.

In the days and weeks that followed, I had to figure out how to keep going, and how to rebuild. It wasn't easy. For a long time, I wasn't sure I wanted to".

"But then, one day, I woke up and realised that if I didn't live, if I didn't move forward, the people who took my husband's life would win. And I couldn't let that happen. I couldn't let them take *everything*."

"That's what this tattoo is about," she said, holding up her wrist. **"Life 2**. It's a reminder. A reminder to never forget what happened, but also a reminder to make the most of this second chance. Not everyone gets one."

For a moment, no one spoke. The weight of her story hung heavy in the air, the table sat in silence. Then, slowly, someone reached out and took her hand. Another hand joined, and another, until everyone at the table was linked.

"To life," someone whispered". "To life," they all echoed, raising their glasses in a solemn toast.

And at that moment, under the soft glow of the city

restaurant, it was clear that her story impacted them all.

She would not know it at the time but her story would be told again on the other side of the world in Melbourne Australia. It was a former news reading colleague and a very close friend of mine who attended that gathering in Boston. He was the one who asked the question 'What happened to Life 1".

As we sipped our lukewarm lattes I watched his eyes mist over as he relived that unforgettable evening.

He agreed with me, everyone has a story to tell if you ask the right question and are prepared to listen.

CHAPTER 4

Princess Diana

A personal conversation – An unexpected confession.

Travelling with toddlers is not for the fainthearted. It is a test of patience, endurance, and sheer willpower. The threat of chaos looms large—screaming babies, leaking nappies, and mid-air tantrums are just the tip of the iceberg. Yet, despite the potential for disaster, parents around the world continue to embark on these journeys, driven by a mix of necessity, adventure, and the hope of creating lasting memories.

As parents of twins, my wife and I experienced our fair share of high-altitude turbulence. While most parents seem to survive these ordeals, some emerge with what could only be described as self-diagnosed PTSD.

Just when we thought the stories couldn't get any worse, they did. But rather than deter us, these tales made us more determined—and more observant of other parents, particularly those in the public eye.

Among the most fascinating examples were visiting Royals. Whenever Prince Charles and Princess Diana emerged from long-distance flights with their young sons, William and Harry, they appeared radiant, regal, and remarkably relaxed.

How did they do it? This question lingered in my mind, especially as we were preparing for a family trip to Disneyland with our twins.

Little did I know that I would soon have the opportunity to seek advice from Princess Diana herself.

Princess Diana was no ordinary Royal. From the moment she stepped into the public eye, she brought

Chapter 4 Princess Diana

a breath of fresh air to the monarchy. Her approach to motherhood was no exception.

In 1983, against the advice of palace officials, Diana made the unprecedented decision to bring Prince William on a six-week tour of Australia and New Zealand.

The tour was a logistical challenge. At the time, Prince William was just nine months old—hardly an ideal age for international travel, let alone a six-week tour filled with endless engagements, photo ops, and gruelling schedules. He was as much the centre of attention as Princess Diana and often left in the care of his nanny at Woomargama, a sheep station near Albury, chosen for its proximity so that the royal couple could fly back to him most nights.

The British press, eager for updates on the young prince, camped outside the farm, desperate for any news or a chance photo. The idea of bringing a baby along on such a demanding trip was unheard of in royal circles, but this tour would be the first for the Royal Couple, Diana and Charles.

Traditionally, royal tours did not include young children. The monarchy sought to avoid the risks associated with travelling with heirs to the throne, fearing that any mishap could threaten the future of the dynasty. But Diana was determined to rewrite the rules. She believed that her role as a mother was just as important as her royal duties, and she was unwilling to sacrifice one for the other.

Despite the challenges, Diana's decision to bring William on the tour was a resounding success. It humanised the royal family, endearing them to the public in a way that no carefully staged photo op ever could.

Five years later, in 1988, the royal family embarked on another tour of Australia, this time with both William and Harry in tow. The tour was part of the Australian Bicentenary celebrations, marking 200 years since the arrival of the First Fleet in 1788 .

The presence of the young princes, particularly William, who was now a toddler and the future heir to the throne, captured the public's imagination. Massive crowds gathered wherever the family went, eager to catch a glimpse of the beloved princess and her boys.

It was during this tour that Prince William celebrated his third birthday, an occasion marked with a happy family image.

But behind the scenes, the image was not all it seemed. Rumours of extramarital affairs had begun to tarnish the family's image, and the strain was evident. Diana, however, remained steadfast in her commitment to her sons. She had familiarised William and Harry with flying from a very early age, beginning with short-distance flights and holidays.

Long-distance flights were something else and never without challenges. Like most young toddlers, William and Harry had moments of frustration and boredom, leading to tears and an occasional mid-flight tantrum. Jet lag, unfamiliar surroundings, and relentless public scrutiny added to an exhausting ordeal in a schedule that often pulled her away for hours at a time.

William was more unsettled than Harry by the constant changes and became fussy and irritable, leading to reports that he wasn't sleeping well, but neither was Diana.

Royal aides urged her to lean on the nannies and staff, but Diana's instincts told her otherwise. She frequently defied protocol, ensuring she had time with her sons—even if it meant sneaking away from official engagements.

Despite the turmoil in their personal lives, Princess Diana was the headline act, winning over the public with her warmth and authenticity. Images of William and Harry also melted Australian hearts. For all the stress and exhaustion, she had proven a point—royal duty didn't come at the cost of motherhood. She represented living proof you can survive travelling with toddlers and that gave us hope that we too could survive travelling with twins. All we needed was some assurance, and it came from Princess Diana herself. What I was not expecting was her reply – a candid and unexpected formula.

Several days after the start of the 1988 royal tour in Melbourne I had the privilege of meeting Prince Charles and Princess Diana at Government House.

Around 250 media representatives gathered in the great hall, where we were given a brief lesson in royal protocol. We were instructed to address Prince Charles as "Sir" and Princess Diana as "Ma'am."

While there were no specific guidelines on topics of conversation, we were reminded to respect the roles of the royal couple.

Less than thirty minutes after the announcement, the room fell into total silence. Moments earlier, it had been alive with the buzz of journalists, editors, and publishers caught up in animated conversation. Now, without warning, all that energy vanished, replaced

Chapter 4 Princess Diana

by an almost palpable stillness. We exchanged puzzled glances, searching for the cause of this sudden shift. And then, we saw her. Princess Diana had entered the room.

I had never before witnessed such an undeniable presence. Charisma is often described as a compelling charm that inspires devotion—a magnetic quality that defies explanation. In that moment, Princess Diana embodied all of those qualities. She didn't demand attention; it was simply given. The atmosphere shifted instantly as if the entire room had been drawn into her orbit. Only later did we learn what made this transformation even more remarkable.

Prince Charles had been in the room for over thirty minutes before her arrival, and none of us had noticed.

I was standing with a small group of Network Ten news staff when Prince Charles approached. Introductions were made, and he immediately engaged with our racing sports reporter, Clem Dimsey, asking about the performance of his horse since his last visit. We were all stunned and impressed by his apparent knowledge and memory of his previous visit. As he moved on to meet the team from GTV9, I overheard his advisor whispering reminders about who was who. "The blond chap is Brian Naylor the senior newsreader, the others are...."

It became clear that he was being fed local knowledge by his living walking, talking autocue.

No sooner had I returned to my team than a soft voice said, "Excuse me, may I join you?" It was Princess Diana.

The first thing I noticed were her sparkling blue eyes, her soft, short blonde hair, and a mischievous, almost shy smile. Our initial conversations revolved around their current tour—its highlights and expectations. Then, the topic turned to children, specifically Princes William and Harry.

Someone mentioned that I was a father of twins, and suddenly, Princess Diana's full attention centred on me.

This was a moment I could never have imagined. After a general discussion about long-distance flights with young children, I posed my well-rehearsed question.

"With all due respect, Ma'am," I began, "may I ask how you cope with travelling with two young toddlers?" Her reply left me momentarily speechless.

"I simply dope them up with Phenergan," she said with a mischievous smile. Did she just admit to sedating her two children?

Perhaps it was my look of shock or disbelief that prompted her to elaborate. "Yes, William tolerates

Phenergan extremely well, but it makes Harry hyper, so we have to lower his dose."

I didn't dare question her pronunciation of the sedative as "Fenner-gun," but the message was clear. I couldn't wait to tell my wife that Phenergan had received the royal stamp of approval, especially since we were about to fly to Disneyland in the United States.

We bought a small bottle of Phenergan, though it remained unopened. Like "Missy" and "Teddy," our twins' favourite security toys, it became our own security blanket. But I will never forget that private conversation with one of the most remarkable people I have ever met.

* * *

After her divorce from Prince Charles, Diana, Princess of Wales, made one final visit to Australia in 1996, a year before her tragic death in 1997.

In 2024, King Charles returned to Australia with Queen Camilla for his first visit as monarch, becoming only the second reigning sovereign to visit the country.

Reflecting on my encounter with Princess Diana, I am still struck by the humanity behind her royal facade. Her candid admission about using Phenergan for her children was a reminder that even those in privileged positions face the same challenges as the rest of us.

The story of royal tours in Australia has left a legacy of pomp and ceremony but the memory of my brief, unforgettable conversation with Princess Diana will last a lifetime.

Additional note.

Australia's drug regulator has issued a safety warning over the use of Phenergan.

The Therapeutic Goods Administration warns the product should not be given to children under the age of six due to concerns of serious side effects, including hyperactivity, aggression and hallucinations.

CHAPTER 5

Miracle at the Crease

'Life After the Boxing Day Tsunami'

Batticaloa, Sri Lanka, 2004.

Boxing Day dawned like any other day in the small fishing village of Batticaloa on the east coast of Sri Lanka. The air was thick with a smoky haze from early morning fires, and the faint scent of saltwater lingered as the villagers began their daily routines. Katina, a 15-year-old local girl, tied her long black hair into a ponytail and kicked off her thongs, preparing to gather driftwood for her stove. Married to Raj and four months pregnant, Katina lived in a shared house just meters from the beach, where the rhythmic sound of the waves was a constant backdrop to her life.

As she ventured onto the mudflats, the early morning sun cast long, speckled shafts of light through the mangroves. The tide was low, and the wet sand glistened underfoot. Katina's ears suddenly popped, as if the air pressure had shifted. She paused, hearing a strange gurgling sound like water being sucked down a drain. Curious, she watched as the tide began to recede at an unnatural speed, faster than she had ever seen before. Fish were left stranded in shallow puddles, flipping and flopping helplessly. Katina hurried to collect them, dropping them into the folds of her floral dress. The fish would be a welcome addition to the driftwood she had already gathered.

But the gurgling sound stopped abruptly, replaced by a low, ominous roar. Katina froze, her instincts screaming at her to run, but it was too late. The ground beneath her feet began to vibrate, and the roar grew

Chapter 5 Miracle at the Crease

louder. A massive wall of water surged toward her, towering over the mangroves. The tsunami hit with unimaginable force, sweeping Katina off her feet and tossing her like a rag doll. The water carried her inland, slamming her into a tree far beyond her home.

The wave receded, only to return with even greater fury. It devoured everything in its path—homes, trees, cars, and people. Katina's house was swept away, along with her husband, Raj. The tsunami left behind a landscape of devastation, mud, and debris.

Miraculously, Katina survived. She was found hours later, unconscious and wedged in the branches of a tree. Rescuers rushed her to the local hospital, where she lay in critical condition for weeks. Her unborn baby, however, appeared unharmed, a small miracle amidst the tragedy.

Katina's survival came at a cost. The trauma left her physically and mentally unable to care for her child. Her parents, already struggling to rebuild their lives, could not support her or the baby. Reluctantly, they made the heart-wrenching decision to put the child up for adoption, believing it was in the baby's best interest.

* * *

We watched in almost disbelief as the harrowing images of the Asian Tsunami streamed into Melbourne's Channel Ten Newsroom. Beside me sat Rabhine, the editor assigned to carefully select the footage that would be appropriate enough for a 5pm news bulletin. Waves swallowing entire villages, debris-strewn landscapes, and the anguished faces of survivors.

Then, something shifted. His composure visibly cracked as he recognised the familiar landscape of his home town region in Sri Lanka.

As a man of Tamil heritage, the weight of the tragedy became too unbearable to continue. "I'm so sorry," he said, "I have to leave... I have to go home to my wife". With tears in his eyes, he slowly stood before quietly closing the door of the editing suite behind him.

Melbourne, Australia, 2014

Nearly a decade later, on a sunny afternoon in a quiet Melbourne suburb, a young boy named Sanjay* stepped onto a cricket pitch. Dressed in pristine whites and padded up, he faced his first ball with the determination of a seasoned player. Though he swung and missed, his parents, Rabhine* and Margarette*, watched from the

---

* Names have been changed to protect Sanjay's identity.

Chapter 5 Miracle at the Crease

sidelines with pride. For them, this moment was more than just a game—it was a testament to the miracle that had brought their son into their lives.

Sanjay's story began on that fateful Boxing Day in 2004 when the Indian Ocean tsunami devastated Sri Lanka and other parts of Southeast Asia. The disaster claimed over 230,000 lives and left countless families shattered. Among the survivors was a baby boy, born into tragedy but destined for a new life.

Rabhine and Margarette, a Tamil couple living in Melbourne, had been married for 15 years but were unable to conceive. Two and a half years before the tsunami, they had applied for adoption, specifically requesting a child from Sri Lanka due to their heritage. The couple had deep ties to their homeland, having worked on village-building projects in the war-torn region.

When the tsunami struck, Rabhine and Margarette were horrified by the scale of the devastation. They mourned the loss of life and the destruction of communities they had worked so hard to rebuild. Little did they know that the tragedy would soon profoundly change their own lives.

Seven months after the tsunami, on July 27, 2005, Rabhine received a phone call from the Victorian

Department of Human Services. The voice on the other end was calm and compassionate but carried a hint of authority. "We would like to inform you that a child has been allocated to you in Sri Lanka," the official said. The news was both thrilling and daunting. The official warned them of the challenges ahead: "If you accept, you will be going to a country where promises are broken, dreams are shattered, and prayers are rarely answered."

Despite the warning, Rabhine and Margarette didn't hesitate. "There was no question we wanted him," Rabhine recalled. Three days later, they boarded a flight to Sri Lanka, detouring through Malaysia to seek blessings from family members.

Their journey was fraught with challenges. Upon arriving in Colombo, they were met by an agent appointed by the Australian government, who briefed them on the adoption process. On August 9, they embarked on a gruelling 300-kilometre road trip to Batticaloa, the epicentre of the tsunami's devastation. The journey took ten hours over rough, underdeveloped roads, some of which had yet to be repaired after the disaster.

When they finally arrived in Batticaloa, they were taken to a 'safe house' where their son was being cared for. It wasn't an orphanage, they were told, but a temporary shelter to protect children from traffickers and other dangers. The baby, just two and a half months old, lay on a bed in a small room.

Rabhine approached the baby cautiously, his hands trembling. "When I first saw him, I couldn't believe it," he said. "I was told to pick him up, and as I carried him across the room, I just burst into tears." Margarette, standing by his side, held him tightly and whispered, "We've got him. We've waited so long for this, and it's finally happened."

The emotional union was brief. They had to leave the baby in the safe house until the adoption was legally finalised. The following day, they were granted permission to take the baby to Colombo for a medical examination required for Australian immigration.

The legal process, however, was far from smooth. On August 12, they returned to Batticaloa for a court appearance, only to be told that the judge was unavailable. The delay was frustrating, but worse was yet to come. That evening, news broke that Sri Lanka's Foreign Minister, Lakshman Kadirgamar, had been assassinated. The country was plunged into a state of emergency, and tensions between the government and the Tamil Tigers escalated.

The next day, the judge finally arrived but was openly hostile to the idea of foreign adoption. He demanded an additional $10,000 in a trust account and grilled Rabhine and Margarette about their personal lives in open court. Despite the humiliation, they agreed to the terms, determined to bring their son home.

On August 14, the judge reluctantly approved the adoption. Relieved but still anxious, Rabhine and Margarette began the long journey back to Colombo with their baby. The roads were lined with military checkpoints, and the atmosphere was tense. At one point, they were ordered out of their car at gunpoint while soldiers searched for weapons.

Back in Colombo, they waited for the final paperwork, including the baby's passport and visa. The city was on edge, with police conducting raids in search of the assassins. On August 21, the visa finally arrived, and they rushed to the airport to catch the first available flight out of the country.

As they approached the immigration counter, their hearts pounded. Sri Lanka had officially opposed foreign adoptions after the tsunami, and they feared their son might be taken from them at the last moment. But the officer stamped their papers without hesitation, and they boarded the plane.

When the wheels finally lifted off the runway, only then did Rabhine and Margarette allow themselves to breathe. They had been through hell, but they had brought back a miracle.

Melbourne, 2014

Nearly ten years later, Sanjay stood at the crease, unaware of the extraordinary events that had brought him to this moment. I turned to Rabhine and asked "Does he know?"

"Not yet". They had decided to wait until the time was right to tell him about his heritage and the miracle of his survival. Though he was clean bowled for six runs, the fact that he was even there was a testament to the resilience of the human spirit and the power of love.

As Rabhine and Margarette watched their son play, they reflected on the journey that had brought them to this point. "We brought back someone who had been blessed in heaven," Rabhine said. For them, Sanjay was not just a son but a symbol of hope and renewal, a reminder that even in the face of unimaginable tragedy, miracles can happen.

CHAPTER 6

Gary Fenton

The Boy from 'Sandy' who shaped Australian Television

September 15th 2000, just 3 hours before the start of what would become the most successful Olympic Games in modern history a lone figure was seen nervously pacing the massive Broadcasting Centre he had created.

Chapter 6 Gary Fenton

This would become the pinnacle of Gary Fenton's 54-year quest to redefine Australian television.

March 5th 2023, nearly 23 years later, a small group of colleagues gathered to remember Gary who had passed away at the age of 80.

It wasn't a flashy affair—just a handful of people whose lives he deeply touched.

There was Bruce McAvaney, Sandy Roberts, Steve Vizard, Bob Campbell; and Brian Ward, the lawyer who'd stood by Gary from the very start.

My wife Pauline was there too—she'd once been Gary's personal secretary, a role that gave her a front-row seat to his amazing skills.

Alongside her were Graeme Rowland and Gordon Bennett, sports production giants who'd helped bring his vision to life.

We sat together, swapping stories about a man who didn't just shape our careers but the industry we were part of.

The stories weren't just about TV—they were about Gary. "Just a boy from Sandy", his home town suburb of Sandringham.

We laughed a lot, we got a little misty-eyed, and we

raised a glass or two to a life that not only influenced ours, but shaped Australian television, captivating millions of viewers.

A Passion for Football:

His childhood friend, lawyer Brian Ward, who was by his side in his final hours, recalled their shared enthusiasm for athletics during their school years in Sandringham. Gary's natural talent for sports was evident early on, and he dreamed of becoming a Victorian Football player. His determination and discipline were unmatched, qualities that would later define his career.

As a schoolboy, Gary joined preseason training sessions at St. Kilda under the legendary coach Alan Jeans. In 1967, he earned recognition for his performance on the field, particularly in a game against the formidable Peter Bedford, where he was named best on the ground. Over time, Gary played 15 games for Sandringham, establishing himself as a skilled wingman known for his speed, courage, and precise ball distribution.

Gary's football career took an exciting turn when he became part of Harry Beitzel's "Galahs", a touring team that included legends like Peter Hudson, Polly Farmer,

Gary Dempsey, and Syd Jackson. During this time, he was coached by a young Ron Barassi, who would later become an icon of the game.

Gary's passion for football briefly took a back seat when he took a gap year and travelled to Kansas, in the USA where he unexpectedly fell in love with NFL football. Immersed in the vibrant world of American sports, he participated in a preseason training camp and witnessed the power of colour television and its impact on sports promotion. This experience would later inspire his ground-breaking career in television.

A Pioneer of Television:

Despite his adventures abroad, in late '69 Gary felt a strong pull to return home. He came back to Melbourne with a renewed sense of purpose: to combine his love of sports with his newfound understanding of television production. His journey into broadcasting began with an unsuccessful interview at GTV9, but Gary was undeterred. Two days later, he approached HSV7 and was hired by Bruce Gyngell, one of Australia's most respected television figures.

Gyngell had just launched the 'Seven Revolution', and Gary quickly became the go-to person for marketing and sales copy. Around the same time, I had joined HSV7, hosting the national game show *Jeopardy* while beginning a cadetship in journalism under the volatile news editor John Maher. It was during this period that Gary and I formed a lasting friendship.

Gary's creativity and ambition knew no bounds. When Seven previewed a new comedy called *Birds of the Bush*, Gary remarked to friends, "It's a shocker—even I could do better." True to his word, he bought a second-hand typewriter, completed a course in comedy writing, and began crafting his own sitcoms. This was just the beginning of his influential career in television programming.

Rising Through the Ranks:

In August 1976, Gary's career took a significant turn when HSV7's program manager, Gordon French, suddenly resigned to move to TCN9 in Sydney. Gary seized the opportunity and threw his hat into the ring for the position. Ten days later, Ron Casey, the general manager, called him back: "You still reckon you want that job? Okay, you got it!" There was no pay rise, but Gary was offered the Holden Premier that French had ordered. It was a modest start, but Gary was ready to prove himself.

Two years later, Gary faced his first major challenge. In September 1978, Seven's star newsreader, Brian Naylor, lost his prime parking spot and stormed out after a heated argument with Ron Casey. Naylor left for Channel Nine, leaving a void in the newsroom. I was approached to take over but initially refused, not wanting the responsibility. Gary, ever the persuasive figure, entered the office with a brochure for the soon-to-be-released Mazda RX7. "Mal, pal, take the job, and this is yours," he said with a grin. I often heard him joke, "Everyone in television has a price. Mal Walden's was an RX7." While not entirely true, it was close enough.

A Legacy of Productions:

As program manager, Gary quickly established his credentials. He strengthened Seven's partnership with Crawford Productions, commissioning new shows like *Against the Wind*, *Cop Shop*, *Skyways*, *A Town Like Alice*, *All the Rivers Run*, *The Shiralee*, and *Shirl's Neighbourhood*. He also championed iconic comedies such as *Acropolis Now* and *Big Girls Blouse*. Under his leadership, Seven's *Penthouse Club* and the legendary *World of Sport* thrived. In 1979, he won a VFL Media Award for commissioning

Mike Brady to write *Up There Cazaly*, which became the unofficial anthem of Aussie Rules.

In the 1980s, Seven was on top of its game. Its news programs, entertainment shows, and football coverage were all highly rated, making HSV7 the undisputed leader in Australian television. However, the rising costs of production led to tensions within the network. During a heated management meeting in Sydney, ATN boss Ted Thomas voiced concerns about the financial strain on programming.

The Rise and Fall of "Neighbours"

One of Gary's most notable achievements was commissioning *Neighbours*, which debuted on 18 March 1985 to positive reviews and strong ratings in Melbourne. However, the show faced challenges in the Sydney market. Conversely, the Sydney-produced drama *Sons and Daughters* struggled in Melbourne but was a hit among Sydney audiences. So, a decision had to be made – one had to go.

On 12 July 1985, Ron Casey was overruled, and Seven announced the cancellation of *Neighbours*. The decision came as a shock to Gary, who was not consulted beforehand. Furious, he packed his desk and left the office. Yet, true to his resilient character, he eventually put the disappointment behind him and moved on.

This marked a pivotal moment in the show's history, but it was far from the end. *Neighbours* would later find new life on Network Ten, becoming one of Australia's most iconic and enduring television series.

Steve Vizard, whose career was propelled by shows like *Fast Forward, Full Frontal*, and *Tonight Live*, credited Gary as "a tireless supporter of Australian talent and Melbourne-based production". "Gary", he said, "had a unique ability to recognise talent and champion ambitious projects, helping to redefine the landscape of Australian television comedy".

Princes of Darkness:

Then came 1987 and the darkest chapter in Gary's career with the failed Fairfax takeover of HSV7. The period was marked by betrayal and loss, as friends and colleagues turned against each other. Gary once confided that it "brought out the worst in all of us". His former colleagues from ATN7 Sydney became known as the "Princes of Darkness", and the takeover lasted 3 months and one day.

It began with the departure of Ron Casey and the

axing of the iconic 'World of Sport'. Staff numbers were reduced, newly acquired equipment was sent back to Sydney, and the football coverage was dropped just weeks before the season opener. A week later, I was called into a meeting and told my services were no longer required. I didn't mind—the place had become a disaster. My emotional on-air farewell became a catalyst for change, and Fairfax eventually withdrew from Melbourne, suffering millions in financial losses.

Gary continued at Seven under Christopher Skase and was duly rewarded for his perseverance. Despite the challenges, he remained a steadfast figure in the industry, contributing to light entertainment specials featuring Rod Stewart, Shirley Bassey, and Barry Humphries.

Gary Fenton's legacy is one of innovation, resilience, and passion. He is remembered as the behind-the-scenes king of Australian sports broadcasting, responsible for bringing free-to-air coverage of rugby league, Test cricket, golf majors, tennis grand slams, and the Bathurst 1000 to Australian audiences. His deep love for Aussie Rules and the Olympics was evident throughout his life, from his coverage of the 1976 Montreal Olympics to the Sydney Games in 2000.

His Lasting Legacy:

In September 1993, Gary Fenton missed his first AFL Grand Final—a significant moment for any Australian football fan. But he had a compelling reason: he was in Monte Carlo for the announcement of the successful bidder for the 2000 Olympic Games. When Juan Antonio Samaranch, President of the International Olympic Committee, uttered the word "Sydney," it marked a turning point in Fenton's life. That announcement would set the stage for a defining moment in his career.

The road to the Sydney Olympics, however, was far from smooth. One of Fenton's first major challenges was securing the television rights for the Games. He found himself up against formidable opponents: Frank Lowy and the team from Ten, the negotiating team from the ABC, and his biggest adversary, media mogul Kerry Packer from the Nine Network. Through a combination of clever negotiation tactics and a fair amount of bluffing, Fenton succeeded in securing the rights for the Seven Network. This victory led to Kerry Packer resigning from the SOCOG Board, another significant win for Fenton and Seven.

While Seven bathed in its Olympic glory Fenton's own position at HSV7 was now uncertain. The network was undergoing more management changes, with Gary Rice appointed as managing director alongside Alan Bateman, one of the infamous 'Princes of Darkness' from the Fairfax takeover. Fenton's contract had expired, and with Bateman in charge, the prospect of an extension seemed unlikely. As Fenton later quoted my wife Pauline "When a door shuts, it's amazing what flies in through the window" and indeed, it did—in the form of a phone call from Monolo Romero, CEO of SOBO, 'How would you like to work for me in Sydney?"

In September 1996, Fenton was appointed Chief Operating Officer of the Sydney Olympic Broadcasting Organisation (SOBO). It was the biggest job in sports television history, and Fenton embraced the challenge with determination. He began assembling a team of proven experts and immediately set out to secure sponsorships. The scale of the task was staggering: over 30 venues spread across Sydney, with a focus on Olympic Park in Homebush Bay, 28 sports, 39 disciplines, and 52 venues to manage. The logistics were overwhelming.

One of the most daunting challenges was sourcing 58 outside broadcast (OB) trucks and control rooms, which had to be transported to Sydney from around the world. The only aircraft capable of handling such a task was a Russian military Antonov, and Fenton's team began negotiations with the USSR military to make it happen. Accommodation was another hurdle. Fenton's team acquired the P&O cruise liner 'Fair Princess' for $1.4 million per day with crew for accommodation.

He also had to address power compatibility issues, as much of the international equipment wasn't suited to Australia's voltage system. Specialised cables and equipment were sourced to power the studios, control rooms, editing suites, and broadcast booths.

Despite the enormity of the task, Fenton's leadership and teamwork prevailed. The Sydney 2000 Olympic Games were hailed as a broadcasting triumph. In a letter from Monolo Romero, he described the coverage as "the best ever" attributing its success to Gary Fenton. Remarkably, the project came in under budget—$191 million against an initial budget of $198 million. How Fenton managed this remains a mystery, but it stands as a testament to his exceptional organizational and financial skills.

Gary Fenton's journey from missing an AFL Grand Final to orchestrating the most ambitious sports broadcasting operation in history is a story of resilience, innovation, and leadership. His work on the Sydney 2000 Olympics not only cemented his legacy but also set a new standard for global sports broadcasting.

As we gathered on Sunday 5 March 2023 to honour our friend one story summed up the tributes and the character of our boy from 'Sandy'. It related to his experience as a young backpacker in the late 60s who had run out of funds while travelling through Europe.

Forced to plead for some money for a meal, he pledged to repay 5 pounds from the total stranger who scribbled his name and address on a piece of paper, not for one moment either believing they would see each other again.

40 years later Fenton fortuitously rediscovered the address while on his way to an International Olympic Committee meeting in Switzerland. During a stopover in London, he withdrew money from the bank and scribbled a note, not knowing if the man was still living at the given address, or even if he was still alive.

'Sorry it's taken so long but here's the quid with interest'. He then posted the note and cash through the slit in the front door and left.

After his IOC meeting in Lausanne he was shocked to discover the 'good Samaritan' Jim Webb, had contacted the BBC who thought it was such a good story it went viral around the world on all news outlets, press, radio and television.

Everyone had a story to tell that day but this one was saved for last.

All too often in life, we are blessed to have personally known those whose contributions have changed the way we live. Sadly, many names become lost in time but their achievements and legacies must survive. That is why we must honour and record their efforts for posterity while we can.

Vale Gary Fenton and thanks to his friend and mentor Bob Campbell for his tribute publication 'Just A Boy From Sandy'.

CHAPTER 7

Munich Massacre

A story of two Australians; one became a media icon, the other became Australian Prime Minister.

It was June 1972, a time of political and social upheaval in Australia. The Australian Council of Trade Unions (ACTU) had just imposed a ban on all French shipping in protest against France's nuclear testing in the Pacific. ACTU President Bob Hawke, a charismatic and controversial figure, was also under intense pressure to ban the forthcoming Springbok Rugby tour as a stand against apartheid in South Africa. However, the West Australian Transport Workers Union and Hotel Industry workers had voted to allow the Rugby players to tour, opening the door for the contentious event.

Amidst this backdrop, rumours began to swirl that Bob Hawke was considering a leap into politics, possibly even vying for leadership of the Labor Party. But his political aspirations were being undermined by his well-documented struggles with alcohol and his womanising. These issues were not only damaging his public image but also straining his relationship with his wife, Hazel, and their family.

It was against this backdrop of breaking news and growing public interest in Bob Hawke that HSV7 Melbourne invited him to appear on its Sunday night current affairs show, *This Week*. The program, hosted by newsreader Brian Naylor, followed the traditional *Meet the Press* format, featuring a panel of journalists from the *Melbourne Herald* who would interview prominent newsmakers of the week.

It was a tradition that every Sunday night, we would gather in the boardroom around 7 o'clock, helping ourselves to plates of sandwiches and preparing to offer our guests a drink or two from the bar fridge. But on this particular night, we discovered that the fridge had been locked by Ron Casey, the station manager. Casey had taken this precaution after a previous incident where the news staff had consumed all the liquor. Undeterred, an enterprising journalist removed the hinges from the fridge door, unlocking a chain of events that would become legendary.

The program was scheduled to be recorded around 8 o'clock and then replayed after the Sunday night movie, which typically aired from 10:30 onward, depending on the film's length. Bob Hawke arrived at the studio accompanied by his wife, Hazel. He was already in high spirits, having clearly indulged in a few drinks beforehand. This was a man who had earned a place in the *Guinness Book of Records* for the fastest time to skol a yard of ale, and it seemed he had been attempting to break his own record that evening. Despite his inebriated state, he was immediately offered another drink, much to Hazel's dismay. She protested, but Hawke snapped at her in a withering tirade, reducing her to tears. Humiliated, Hazel left the studio and was driven back to their Sandringham home by one of the cameramen.

As tensions mounted, Hawke was ushered into the studio, and the program began on schedule. Brian Naylor introduced his guest and the panel of interviewers. What followed was a vintage Bob Hawke performance. He dismantled each questioner with sharp, cutting remarks. "What sort of question is that? I would expect more from you... You call yourself a journalist? You're not a journalist's bootlace!" and that set the tone for the rest of the interview.

However, the program never made it to air. Twenty-eight years later, Ron Casey, confided in me at a corporate lunch what had happened that night—and how he may have inadvertently saved Bob Hawke's political career.

Casey began his story:

"It was Sunday, June 4, 1972. I was sitting at home when I received a call around 9:30 from Sandra Fitzell, the producer of *This Week*. She said, 'Ron, I have a problem. The program is complete, but our guest, Mr. Hawke, is drunk. He's slandered and slurred his way through the show, and I don't know what to do. Naylor is demanding we run it, but I have my doubts.'"

Casey knew the program would make for sensational

television, but he also understood the potential repercussions for both the station and Bob Hawke. After careful consideration, he decided to destroy the recording and replace it with a movie. The following day, Casey received a phone call from a very contrite Bob Hawke. "Ron," Hawke said, "I want to apologise for my behaviour last night and thank you for the action you took. I owe you one, I really do."

Three months later, Ron Casey left for Munich. The Seven Network had secured shared rights to broadcast the 1972 Summer Olympics in Australia, a ground-breaking event that would be the first Olympic Games streamed around the world in vivid colour. Although colour television had not yet been launched in Australia, special arrangements had been made at the HSV7 studios in South Melbourne to accommodate sponsors and media buyers, allowing them to witness the historic live colour feed before it was re-transmitted in black and white.

However, just as the Olympic athletes were about to file into the stadium for the opening ceremony, Melbourne's postal technicians went on strike, severing the video link from Munich. Panic erupted from the master control centre in Melbourne to the

Chapter 7 Munich Massacre

Olympic broadcast centre in Munich. Amid the chaos, Ron Casey remained calm.

"I simply picked up the phone in Munich and called Bob Hawke at his home in Melbourne," Casey recalled. "I said, 'Bob, I have a problem... and you owe me a favour.'"

According to Casey, Hawke slammed the phone down, jumped into his car, and drove directly into the city. He burst into the telecommunications centre and physically pushed the plug into the socket himself, reconnecting the Olympic studios in Munich to the television studios in South Melbourne with just minutes to spare. Thanks to Hawke's quick action, HSV7 did not lose a single second of the opening coverage or a dollar of sponsors' fees. Or so the story goes.

In Munich, Ron Casey wasn't the only one breathing a sigh of relief. Judy Patching, the Olympic chef de mission and Victoria's Olympic team boss, was so impressed by Casey's calm demeanour and the seamless coverage of the opening ceremony that he handed Casey his personal phone number. "Judy scribbled the number on the back of a business card and stuffed it into the top pocket of my reefer jacket. Call me anytime. It's the direct number to my room." But then I forgot all about it."

Two nights later, Casey was woken by a phone call in his hotel room. It was Sandra Fitzell, the news producer, back in Melbourne. "What can you tell me about the Olympic massacre?" she asked.

"I sat there stunned as Sandra told me that Arab terrorists had killed several Israeli athletes and taken others hostage," Casey recalled. "I told her I would call her back, hung up, and immediately fumbled for the business card Judy Patching had given me. I called his number, and he answered almost immediately. 'Come straight to my room,' he said. 'I have the sole eyewitness with me.'

As all international journalists were scrambling for exclusive eyewitness accounts, Ron Casey, found himself at the centre of the story.

* * *

It was shortly after 4 a.m. on September 5, 1972, when eight heavily armed members of Black September, a faction of the Palestine Liberation Organisation (PLO), scaled the perimeter fence of the Olympic Village and made their way to the building housing Israeli officials. Disguised in tracksuits, they stormed the first apartment, where two Israeli athletes tried to block the door. The terrorists forced their way in, killing both men in the struggle. A third athlete managed to escape by fighting off a terrorist and fleeing into the night.

The terrorists then stormed another apartment, taking nine Israeli athletes and coaches hostage. They demanded the release of 234 Palestinian prisoners and two German extremists.

Among the first eyewitness accounts were those attributed to British silver medalist swimmer David Wilkie, who, along with two teammates, had been returning to the Olympic Village after a night out. They had seen two people in tracksuits climbing over the perimeter fence and assumed they were athletes. It was the beginning of the attack.

An Israeli survivor Shaul Ladany, described how his roommate had woken him, claiming that their teammate, Weinberg, had been shot and killed. Ladany dressed and left the room, half-expecting to see a war zone outside their apartment. "The first person I spotted was a member of the terror squad wearing what I thought was an Australian hat," Ladany said. "He was talking to four unarmed village guards and a lady who was pleading, 'You must let the Red Cross in; be humane.' The terrorist simply replied, 'The Jews are not humane.'"

Negotiations with German authorities lasted hours, but the situation deteriorated rapidly. The hostages and terrorists were flown to Fürstenfeldbruck airbase, where a poorly planned rescue operation ended in disaster. German police, outnumbered and outgunned, failed to contain the terrorists. A firefight broke out, and ended when the terrorists detonated a grenade inside the rescue helicopter, killing the remaining hostages. By the end of the ordeal, all 11 Israeli athletes, one German police officer, and five terrorists were dead.

The Black September attack and the botched rescue attempt were broadcast live, marking the first time a terrorist attack was reported in real-time. Ron Casey, who had initially been in Munich to cover the Olympics, found himself thrust into the role of a journalist, securing the first eyewitness accounts of the tragedy.

Ron Casey would later attribute much of his media success to his profile born out of the tragic events that unfolded in Munich.

He went on to cover nine more Olympic Games, became a key figure in the Australian Olympic

Committee, and played a significant role in lobbying for Melbourne's Olympic bid.

He was promoted from station manager to general manager of HSV7 and served on the Board of the Federation of Australian Commercial Television Stations.

He became a board member of the North Melbourne Football Club.

His contributions to journalism and sports were recognized with numerous accolades, including an MBE for services to journalism and the Order of Australia (AM) for services to sport.

Reflecting on his career over a lunch at Melbourne's RACV Club, Casey joked that much of his success might never have happened had Bob Hawke not got drunk that night in 1972.

On March 11, 1983, Bob Hawke was sworn in as Australia's 23rd Prime Minister. His leadership would be remembered for its economic reforms, social progress, and his ability to connect with everyday Australians.

The story of Bob Hawke and Ron Casey is one of redemption, resilience, and the unpredictable ways in which lives and histories intertwine. Then came Moscow, and under another PM the greatest test of Casey's resilience and leadership.

Moscow Olympic Drama

Three days before New Year's Eve 1979, Russian tanks and troops rolled into Afghanistan.

So began a fateful incursion that would cost over two million lives and embroil the Soviet Union in a ten-year war, a war they wouldn't win. The repercussions were felt worldwide and nowhere would the situation be more resolutely tested than at the studios of HSV7 in Melbourne.

The US branded the invasion as the greatest threat to world peace since the Second World War. The Western world was united in its condemnation and leading the charge was Australia's PM Malcolm Fraser. The looming Olympics in Moscow suddenly became a political issue. Pressure was being applied on local Olympic Federations to boycott the Moscow Games. The US, Canada, West Germany and Japan bowed to the pressure and announced they would not be sending teams.

The Australian Olympic Federation was split down the middle. Some were angry at what they perceived was the PM's meddling in sport. Others believed it was morally wrong to recognise so prominently a nation that was so brutally invading another. The community

was polarised. Even the athletes became involved with Olympic veteran Herb Elliott urging Australia to boycott, while
swimming legend Dawn Fraser warned a boycott would destroy the Olympic movement. Eventually, it came down to a vote. Olympic chiefs would meet to make a final decision on whether Australian athletes would attend the Moscow Games.

The day arrived and nowhere was the tension greater than it was at HSV7 in Melbourne. Ron Casey paced the corridors. His face was flushed as he continually scratched his already inflamed and blotchy skin. He nervously checked teleprinter reports, constantly accompanied by the equally nervous executives Howard Gardner and Gary Fenton. There was much at stake as Casey and Fenton had personally negotiated an exclusive rights deal; the first 'exclusive rights' for the Seven network to broadcast an Olympic Games. It was an agreement secured after a secret tip-off by an unknown member of the Australian Olympic Committee that Kerry Packer was about to fly to Moscow in a bid to secure the deal for the Nine network. Within hours of being tipped off Casey flew to Moscow, outmanoeuvring Packer at the last moment.

Such was the intensity and interest in the decision for Australia to compete in the Moscow Olympics that the vote was to be broadcast live on the ABC. Millions of dollars in network sponsorship was at stake. Millions of dollars in technology had been assembled. The nation may have been divided, but Channel Seven was totally in support of the Games going ahead. Never had so much interest been concentrated on a single radio broadcast. Then, as the vote was finally announced, there was an almighty scream from Casey's office, followed by pandemonium and celebrations among the staff. The decision was made 6-5 to go to Moscow.

Within days, Ron Casey received a deputation from PM Malcolm Fraser. The PM arrived at the Station in Dorcas Street, South Melbourne, accompanied by Liberal Party President, Tony Eggleton and his Foreign Affairs Minister, Andrew Peacock.

According to those present, the meeting lasted just 90 seconds.

Malcolm Fraser had been politely ushered into Casey's office. They immediately dispensed with all pleasantries and the PM began with what all described was a well-rehearsed dialogue.

Fraser cut straight to the chase, outlining the

morality of recognising the Soviet regime, which he said was carrying out a brutal scorched earth campaign against innocent civilians in Afghanistan. He barely took breath as he continued his support for a boycott and the need to join the other Western nations, which 'had so rightly and justly decided to boycott the Games to show support for the oppressed people of Afghanistan'. He was about to continue when Ron Casey interrupted.

'With all due respect Mr Prime Minister, may I suggest you run the country and I will run this television station.'

There was a pause. With a look of almost stunned disbelief in his eyes, Fraser then turned on his heels and stormed out with Eggleton and Peacock right behind.

That night Casey, Fenton and several senior executives went out to celebrate the outcome of the vote. They booked a table at Maxim's restaurant in Toorak Road, South Yarra. Around 11 p.m. after most guests had left, the door of a private room, adjoining the main dining room suddenly opened. Striding through the door was the PM and several guests. Malcolm Fraser immediately walked up to Ron Casey and placed a bottle of port on the table.

'Ron,' he said, 'I'm just dropping Tammie home. We are only just around the corner; I'll be back in five minutes.'

Keeping to his word he returned and while they spoke briefly about the day's events and the boycott vote, they drank until 3 a.m. Neither side backed down from their position, but Casey said he had a much greater appreciation for the PM than earlier in the day.

Casey left a legacy in sport and the television industry of which he was most proud. I have always believed it's not what you know, it's who you know in life and I too was so proud to have been a witness to his many contributions.

The last time I saw Case (as we affectionately called him) was at our luncheon, in October 1999 where he reflected on the terrible tragedy of the Munich Games.

He died on 19 June the following year.

CHAPTER 8

Miracle In The Andes

A personal insight into one of the most harrowing and inspiring tales of survival in modern history.

Nando Perrado

On 14 October 1972, I was in the Channel Seven newsroom when the bell on the teleprinter suddenly rang out. I ripped off the message, which read *'Fears for Rugby Team'* (stop). *'Plane missing in the Andes (stop)*'. As Channel Seven was Melbourne's football station, the producer agreed the story would resonate with our viewers. It was not the lead story but placed high in the rundown.

Throughout the following week, we kept abreast of the story but as hopes began to fade and the search for survivors was called off, the story faded from prominence.

By pure coincidence, I was on duty 72 days later when the bells again rang out. The message simply stated "Alive" and we all immediately knew what it referred to.

On 11th August 2014 , the leading survivor of that crash, Nando Perrado, who had become one of the world's most sought-after inspirational public speakers, was invited to talk to members of Melbourne's Carlton Football Club and I was asked to introduce him.

I was perhaps one of the few guests who had been aware of his extraordinary story from the very start.

After my brief explanation and against a background screen of actual news footage, Nando told his story.

Alive (Nando's Story)

"It was October 13, 1972, probably a day before you first heard it on the news here in Australia, when the

Chapter 8 Miracle In The Andes

chartered twin-engine plane carrying the Uruguayan Rugby Team was on the final leg of our journey to play an exhibition game in Chile, Santiago. Most of the 45 people on board were in their late teens and early 20s. There were some parents of players, some supporters and my mother and sister Susie".

"The trouble began when the pilot believed he had cleared The Andes and had been given instructions to commence his descent. The problem was he had become disorientated due to bad weather and poor visibility and was still above the Alps. No one on board appeared concerned. Some even whooped and hollered when we hit some turbulence. The plane had entered thick fog. The steward told us to fasten our seatbelts as severe turbulence struck. We hit another air pocket and dropped what felt like hundreds of feet.

Suddenly, we fell beneath the cloud cover and my colleague pointed out the window to a mountain peak just 10 or 20 feet away".

"Is it normal to fly so close, he asked"? "I don't think so, I replied, with a frightening knot in my stomach". Then there was this sudden crash and my world turned upside down and everything faded to black".

The plane had hit the mountain. The impact was

devastating. The wings were torn off, and the fuselage slid down the slope before coming to a stop at the end of a ravine. Nando was knocked unconscious, and for 2 days Iay in a coma suffering severe head injuries.

"The first thing I remember as I emerged from unconsciousness were voices. "Nando, are you OK? Nando, are you OK?" I was not OK. I looked around a tangled fuselage that had rolled onto its side. The damage was catastrophic: exposed pipes and cables, crumpled metal, shattered plastic, and wreckage everywhere".

"I pressed the side of my head, clumped with clotted blood, and felt the edges of splintered bone. My friend Roberto Canessa explained the plane had hit a mountain three days before and I had been unconscious since. My immediate thoughts turned to my mother and sister Susie".

"It was then I was told, Nando, your mother is dead and your sister is not expected to survive. Susie was gravely injured, lying on the floor by the cockpit. She couldn't talk. She could only move her eyes. She lost her shoes in the crash and her feet were purple. Those are the images that I have. I stayed with her. I melted snow with my mouth and gave her water because we didn't have anything. We didn't have cups".

Chapter 8 Miracle In The Andes

The initial crash killed 12 people and left a number of the 33 surviving passengers injured.

In the days that followed, they struggled to come to terms with their new reality. They were stranded in the middle of the Andes, with no food, no shelter, and no way to call for help. The cold was relentless, and the nights were the worst. They huddled together in the wreckage of the plane, trying to stay warm, but it was never enough. Every morning, they woke up to find that someone else had died in the night.

10 days after the crash they heard on a transistor radio salvaged from the wreckage that the search efforts had been called off and they knew from that moment no one was coming to save them.

"If we were going to survive, we would have to do it ourselves. But how? The mountains were vast and unforgiving, and we had no idea where we were or how to get out".

"The biggest challenge was food. We had a few chocolate bars and some canned food, but it wasn't enough to sustain us. We tried to ration what we had, but it was clear that we would soon run out. Then, one day, someone suggested the unthinkable: we would have to eat the bodies of the dead to survive".

"The idea was horrifying. We were all raised in Catholic families, and the thought of cannibalism went against everything we believed in. But what choice did we have? It was either that or die. We made a pact: if any of us died, the others would use our bodies to stay alive.

It was a decision born out of desperation, but it was the only way. We treated the unthinkable as communion".

Just when they thought things couldn't get worse, they did. On the 17th day, an avalanche roared down and buried the fuselage. Nando was outside at the time and watched in horror as the snow came crashing down. He tried to run, but it was too late. The snow engulfed him and he was briefly buried alive.

"I don't know how long I was under the snow, but it felt like an eternity. I couldn't move, couldn't breathe. I thought I was going to die. But then, somehow, I managed to dig myself out. I was alive, but the fuselage was completely buried. I screamed for help, and slowly, one by one, the others began to emerge from the snow. But not everyone made it. Eight more people had died in the avalanche, including some of my closest friends".

"The avalanche broke us. We had already been through

so much, and now this. I felt like giving up. What was the point of fighting anymore? But then I thought of my father. He was waiting for me at home, and I couldn't let him down. I had to survive, no matter what".

As the weeks passed by, their situation became more desperate. They were running out of food, and the cold was taking its toll. They knew they couldn't stay in the mountains forever. If they were going to survive, they would have to find a way out. They were reduced to talk in whispers to conserve energy.

"Roberto Canessa and I began talking about journeying to find help. We knew it would be dangerous—we had no maps, no equipment, and no idea where we were going—but we had no other choice. We decided that we would head west, toward Chile. We didn't know how far it was, but we had to try".

"Before we left, I went to say goodbye to my mother and sister. I knelt beside their bodies in the snow and told them that I loved them. I promised them that I would make it home, no matter what. It was the hardest thing I've ever had to do".

They both set out on December 12, 1972 carrying a small supply of dried meat, a few pieces of clothing, and a sleeping bag made from the plane's insulation.

They had no idea what lay ahead, but were determined to keep going.

The journey was brutal. The mountains were steep and treacherous, and the cold was relentless. They climbed for hours.

They talked about their families, their dreams, and their hopes for the future. "It was those conversations that kept us going".

"After 10 days of walking, we finally reached the top of a mountain. From there, we could see a valley below. Desperately, uncertainly, we picked our way down the mountain and began to stumble along the glacier down below, trying to force ourselves onward but weakening day by day until, on December 18, we heard rushing water. It was the mouth of a river, which we began to follow. The next day we saw signs of humanity: a rusted soup can, a horseshoe, cow dung, a herd of cows.

Finally, on the evening of December 20, we saw a man on horseback on the other side of the river".

"The following day three more appeared but we were unable to make ourselves heard above the roar of the river, to explain who we were, even miming an airplane crashing fearing he may think were lunatics and leave.

Instead, one of the men tied a note to a rock and threw it across the river: "Tell me what you want." My hands were shaking, as I began writing: "I come from a plane that fell into the mountains."

"We explained that we were weak and starving, that 14 friends remained on the plane, and that they needed help desperately soon. The man read it and raised his hands as if to say, "I understand." Then he immediately left on horseback.

Within hours, they heard the throb of approaching choppers. The Chilean rescue helicopters landed, and although at first the crews and mounted police clearly doubted their story of scaling and descending the mountain, they soon boarded the rescue helicopter in search of the plane.

"As I flew over the mountains, I looked down at the wreckage I couldn't help thinking of my mother, sister and all the friends we had lost. They were gone, but we had survived. We had made it".

At a hospital in San Fernando, Chile, Nando was relieved of his layers of filthy clothing and given a warm shower. It was then he caught a glimpse of himself in a mirror and was shocked at the skin and bones, a shadow of his former self when he boarded the plane two and a half months previously.

"But, with each breath, I kept repeating two words "I'm alive. I'm alive. I'm alive."

In the years that have followed, Nando Perrado has shared his story with the world and on this night it was our turn in Melbourne.

"My name is Nando Parrado, and this is my story, a story of survival, of resilience, and of the unbreakable will to live. I share with you that even in the darkest of times, there is always hope".

* * *

I then opened it up to a Q&A. The first question is "Do you still catch up with fellow survivors?".

'Yes', he replied with a slightly mischievous smile, 'each year we hold a barbeque'.

Soon after the rescue of the 16 survivors, Nando worked with Piers Paul Read, who penned the best-selling book *Alive*. Twenty years later, a film of the same name was released, starring Ethan Hawke as Nando. Nando is himself, the author of the New York Times bestseller *Miracle in the Andes: 72 Days on the Mountain and My Long Trek Home*. He is also a successful businessman and television producer.

Nando Perrado proudly admits he was the creator of the popular car show 'Top Gear' which was picked up by the BBC a year later. But that story I suspected was one he wasn't too happy to talk about. An opportunity lost.

CHAPTER 9

Idi Amin

Creating a Media Myth

Africa's most brutal dictator.

Everyone has a story to tell, though not all want to claim the credit. Some stories linger in your mind, not because they are grand or life-altering, but because they reveal something deeply unsettling about the world we live in. This is one of those stories.

Chapter 9 Idi Amin

It's a tale about how a myth was born, how it spread, and how it became part of history—not because it was true, but because it was intriguing. It's also a story about trust, secrecy, and the weight of an agreement I made to a man whose name I promised never to reveal.

* * *

It was one of those quiet days in the newsroom at Network Ten in Melbourne. The kind of day when the world seems to pause, and the usual chaos of politics, crime, and disaster takes a brief respite. The silence felt almost too calm as if it were waiting to be broken by something extraordinary. That's when my colleague pulled me aside. He had a story to tell, one he had kept hidden for years. But before he began, he made me swear never to reveal his identity. I agreed, not knowing he was about to confess to creating arguably one of the world's great myths surrounding the despotic Ugandan leader Idi Amin—the accusation that he was a cannibal.

"It was," he confided, "born out of a boozy night, a stale pizza, and a mouldy piece of meat."

His story began in London in the mid-1970s, when two

Australian journalists, both of dubious backgrounds, packed their bags for a two-month stint overseas. They had grand plans of writing a book, something sensational that would capture the public's imagination and, more importantly, pay their bills. They moved into a below-ground bedsit apartment in a seedy part of Earl's Court, an area colloquially known as "Kangaroo Valley" due to its large Australian expat population.

Both men were seasoned journalists, having cut their teeth at Melbourne's notorious 'Truth' newspaper and 'The Sunday Observer'. They were what you might call "hack journalists"—men who could churn out stories with minimal facts and maximum flair. They weren't interested in deep investigative reporting; they wanted quick, sensational stories that would sell. And they had their sights set on Idi Amin, the infamous Ugandan dictator.

Since he seized power in a military coup in 1971, Idi Amin had become one of Africa's most brutal leaders.

His rule was defined by widespread human rights abuses. He targeted ethnic groups, political opponents, and intellectuals, leading to the deaths of an estimated 500,000 Ugandans. Many more were tortured or simply disappeared.

Chapter 9 Idi Amin

In 1972, Amin expelled Uganda's Asian community, confiscating their businesses and devastating the economy.

Amin's eccentricity and megalomania were also evident in his self-proclaimed titles, such as "President for Life" and "Conqueror of the British Empire".

His life story was one of ego, brutality and unsubstantiated myths. So, they thought, why not add another myth to his life?

There was no shortage of material to work with. Amin's atrocities were well-documented, and the press releases and media reports which kept coming out of Africa, provided ample fodder for their book. But as the days turned into weeks and their money began to run out, so too did their ideas. They were stuck, staring at a blank page, with nothing but a second-hand typewriter and a dwindling supply of alcohol to keep them going.

Then, one evening, in a haze of booze and desperation, my colleague went to the fridge in search of sustenance. All that was left were a few cold stubbies of beer, a stale pizza, and a mouldy piece of steak. He eyed the steak and suddenly yelled, "Eureka!" They would turn Idi Amin into a cannibal, feasting on one of his enemies. It was a tasteless joke, born out of desperation and alcohol, but it stuck.

They began to weave the idea into their book, crafting scenes where Amin feasted on his enemies, his appetite for human flesh as insatiable as was his thirst for power. It was fiction, of course, but they presented it as fact, knowing that the sensational claim would sell copies.

Within a short time, their project was complete.

The next challenge was finding a publisher. They approached a minor publishing house, one that was willing to take a chance on their manuscript for a modest sum. The payment was just enough to cover their rent and buy another round of drinks. What they didn't realise was that their book would become a victim of syndication.

In the 1970s, the media landscape was very different from what it is today. News stories were often syndicated through networks like the Underground Press Syndicate (UPS), which allowed countercultural newspapers and magazines to reprint each other's content. This created a fertile ground for myths and misinformation to spread, especially when they aligned with existing stereotypes or preconceived notions. The story of Amin's cannibalism fitted perfectly into the narrative of the "savage African dictator".

By the time the claim reached mainstream media, it had taken on a life of its own. There was no way of stopping its circulation, nor was there any way for the journalists to reap further rewards. Much to their relief, their names had been lost in the paper trail of edits and syndication. The myth had escaped their control, and there was no turning back.

In 1976 their story took a back seat when one of the most internationally notorious events during Amin's rule took place. Palestinian and German hijackers seized an Air France plane, diverting it to Entebbe airport in Uganda where over 100 Israeli and Jewish passengers were held hostage. In a daring rescue mission, Israeli commandos stormed the airport, freeing nearly all the hostages and dealing a humiliating blow to Amin's ego. However, one of the passengers, 74-year-old Dora Bloch, an Israeli/ British citizen, had been taken to hospital after choking on a chicken bone. After the raid, she was seen screaming as she was being removed from the hospital by Ugandan Army officers and executed.

By 1979, a series of other books had also been

published, all repeating the claim that this brutal dictator was a cannibal. Some went into graphic detail, describing his supposed appetite for human flesh in lurid prose. The myth had become so widespread that it was accepted as fact, even though there was no evidence to support it. Amin himself never addressed the claim, perhaps because he knew that denying it would only lend it more credibility.

Amin's reign came to an end in 1979 when he fled Uganda and sought refuge first in Libya and then in Saudi Arabia.

He lived in Jeddah, surrounded by his wives, children, and grandchildren, until he died in 2003. His friend, King Faisal, ensured that he was well-provided for, supplying him with alcohol and cannabis to keep his temper in check and protecting him from multiple charges of murder, rape, and corruption. He died at the age of 78, leaving behind a legacy of brutality—and a myth that persists to this day.

My colleague has also passed away, and with him went confirmation about how the cannibalism myth was born. I have kept my promise to protect his anonymity, but the story has lived on, a reminder of how easily fiction can masquerade as fact.

The story of Idi Amin's cannibalism is a cautionary tale, a reminder that myths can become legitimate news and warp our sense of history.

The story of Idi Amin's cannibalism is not just about one man or one myth; it's about the power of media to shape our understanding of history. In the decades since Amin's rule, scholars and journalists have revisited the cannibalism claim, finding no credible evidence to support it. Yet, the myth persists, a testament to the enduring power of sensationalism.

If there's a lesson to be learned from this story, it's that we must be vigilant about the information we consume and the narratives we accept as truth. The media has the power to shape our understanding of the world, but it is also susceptible to manipulation and sensationalism.

The story of Idi Amin's cannibalism created a myth born out of historical curiosity and nothing more than a stale pizza and mouldy piece of meat. Or did it?

CHAPTER 10

A Lethal Legacy

Trevor Grant.

'Hush money and coverups as asbestos cancer strikes media-workers'.

This is a personal tribute following a chance encounter with an old friend and his final words that will live with me forever.

"Mate, I have to tell you I'm dying. I have a disease I can't pronounce (peritoneal mesothelioma), born in a dusty town in Western Australia, I have never been to".

Chapter 10 A Lethal Legacy

Shocked at the news, I searched to find the right words while trying to comprehend my friend's tragic news and the impact it must be having on his life. Or what was left of it?

We had formed a friendship in the late 1960s when he was pursuing an early career in newspapers and I was working in radio at 3DB. Both were part of the monolithic Herald and Weekly Times. Over the years, Trevor Grant became one of Melbourne's leading sports writers, his byline gracing the pages of 'The Age' and 'The Herald'. Always passionate, articulate, and deeply committed to his craft.

Now our paths had coincidentally crossed again. In our retirement years, I became involved in the Balibo Trust, a foundation formed in memory of five colleagues killed by Indonesian troops in East Timor in 1975.

Trevor became the convenor of the Tamil Refugee Council, providing support and advocacy for Tamil refugees and raising awareness about human rights abuses in Sri Lanka.

Now he was about to raise awareness of another issue; one that would claim his life and threaten the lives of thousands of Australians, including veteran media workers such as himself.

We were both leaving a charity function when he pulled me aside. He was eager to talk, like a kettle on the boil where the automatic switch had failed to turn off, and his story all poured out.

"It all came from nowhere. A short, sharp pain in the right shoulder while carrying a full shopping bag, a trip to the GP, an X-ray that revealed a shadow on the lining of my lung, a couple of further scans, and presto, there I was, sitting before a specialist at a Box Hill hospital as he told me: "I'm sorry to have to tell you that you have cancer... mesothelioma"

"There must be some mistake", I thought," Mesothelioma victims were easily defined as plumbers, electricians, or builders – not journalists". "As a journalist who had worked for 40 years on Melbourne's two main newspaper companies, The Age and the Herald, I felt I just didn't fit the bill".

But the reality was far more insidious. Trevor's oncologist explained that mesothelioma could lie dormant in the body for decades, showing no symptoms until it was too late. From his experience, the likely breeding ground for this silent killer was his place of work, the newspaper organisations.

The revelation was devastating. Trevor had spent

his career in what he believed was a safe environment, only to learn that he had been exposed to this killer virus. His anger was palpable, but it was tempered by a profound sadness.

Determined to understand how this had happened, Trevor sought answers. It was only after contacting the legal firm Slater and Gordon that he discovered the tentacles of this terrible disease were spreading far and wide through the community, to a point where it was no longer correct to describe it as rare.

Through a Supreme Court action he launched in 2015, he discovered that the buildings where he had worked—'The Age' at 250 Spencer Street and 'The Herald' office on Flinders Street—were contaminated with asbestos.

Records showed workers in both these buildings, mostly printers and tradesmen working with insulation, had contracted mesothelioma during these times. Printing machines with gaskets and rollers, particularly in Linotype insulation, utilised extremely high amounts of asbestos.

While he worked on separate floors, he had regular contact with these individuals, especially during his early years as a sub-editor.

"I discovered dangers from asbestos had been around for decades, both at The Age, where I worked from 1969-1970 and 1978-1989, and the Herald, where I worked from 1970-74 and 1989-1996".

From the obvious construction industry, automotive and commercial industries, the insidious effects have silently crept into everyday home appliances. From early model television receivers and filters in early-model hair dryers to gaskets and sealers in the plumbing and electrical industries.

Today, the threat continues with warnings to DIY home renovators where asbestos served as home insulation.

"I expected to be angry about all this," he said. "Angry about a cynical corporation risking so many thousands of lives, including my own, for the sake of its bottom line. Angry that nobody warned potential victims that they had worked in places where others had contracted the disease. But all I feel is sadness—sadness that I live in a society that, so often and so easily, writes off human lives as collateral damage in the pursuit of profit." And anger at the pressure on so many in the industry forced into non-disclosure agreements in return for compensation".

The Age and Herald, along with the infamous makers of asbestos-riddled products, James Hardie, agreed to settle his case out of court, which included a significant payout. In legal terms, this was not an admission of guilt by any of them. But Trevor was angry and determined that his story would not be swept under the carpet, despite non-disclosure threats, as was the case with many before him.

Now his story is out, and among his final words, he simply said, 'Above all else, I just want to die happy.'

Trevor Grant died on 5 March 2017.

* * *

Trevor's story cannot be separated from the broader tragedy of asbestos-related diseases in Australia, a crisis born in the scorched landscape of Wittenoom, Western Australia. Once a proud, thriving hub of blue asbestos mining, Wittenoom is now a ghost town, its streets abandoned with land so contaminated that it ranks among the world's most hazardous sites, comparable to the Chernobyl nuclear disaster or India's Bhopal gas catastrophe.

For those who lived and worked there, Wittenoom's

legacy is personal—a story of loss, illness, and betrayal. It's a stark reminder of the human cost of corporate greed and the enduring fight for accountability.

In 1943, the Colonial Sugar Refining Company (CSR) took control of Wittenoom's asbestos mines through its subsidiary, Australian Blue Asbestos Ltd., extracting the highly toxic blue asbestos used in construction, manufacturing, and countless other applications. At its peak, Wittenoom was a bustling community, home to thousands of workers and their families, all drawn by the promise of prosperity. But this prosperity was built on a deadly lie. Mining operations released clouds of asbestos dust into the air, exposing miners, their families, and even casual visitors to its toxic fibres.

Despite warnings about the health risks of asbestos dating back to the 1920s, CSR dismissed the dangers, assuring workers that the dust was harmless. Safety measures were virtually non-existent, and the consequences were catastrophic.

By the 1950s, the human toll was impossible to ignore. Residents and workers began falling ill with asbestosis, lung cancer, and mesothelioma, their lives cut short by diseases that could have been prevented. Yet mining continued, driven by the relentless pursuit of profit.

Chapter 10 A Lethal Legacy

In 1957, CSR partnered with James Hardie Industries, which used Wittenoom's asbestos to produce building materials like roofing, insulation, and fibro sheeting. These products spread the danger far beyond the town, embedding asbestos in homes, schools, workplaces, and public buildings across Australia. The mine finally closed in 1966, not out of concern for public health, but because it was no longer economically viable.

By then, thousands had been exposed, and many were already on a path to premature death, their fates sealed by the fibres lodged in their lungs.

The fight for justice began in the 1980s, when the true scale of the tragedy started to emerge.

In a landmark 1988 case, CSR was found guilty of "reckless indifference" for knowingly endangering workers, a ruling that opened the door for victims to seek compensation.

But the road to justice was fraught with obstacles. Companies like James Hardie employed tactics to evade responsibility, including relocating to the Netherlands in 2001 to shield themselves from liability.

Victims and their families faced protracted legal battles, often compounded by the emotional and financial strain of terminal illness. For many, the compensation they received came with strings attached—confidentiality clauses that silenced their stories and protected the corporations from further scrutiny.

The scale of the tragedy is almost incomprehensible. In the most recent survey, asbestos-related diseases have claimed 45,200 lives in Australia. It's also estimated that over 4000 Australians will die annually from the effects of asbestos, and this statistic is rising. Some experts warn that by 2030, the toll could exceed 60,000, cementing a legacy of Australia having the highest rate of Asbestos-related deaths in the world.

The victims are not just those who worked in the mines or factories; they include people like Trevor Grant, whose exposure came from workplaces they believed were safe. Countless other lives have been touched by asbestos in homes, schools, or public spaces.

The courage of individuals like Trevor Grant and campaigners like Bernie Banton AM has been instrumental in securing justice for victims. Banton, a working-class hero who himself succumbed to peritoneal mesothelioma in 2007, became the face of the fight against James Hardie, exposing the company's callous disregard for workers' lives. His advocacy, alongside legal victories, forced corporations to confront their culpability, though many victims still face barriers to justice. The pressure to sign non-disclosure agreements, as Trevor experienced, remains a significant obstacle, perpetuating a cycle of secrecy that protects the guilty and denies closure to the afflicted.

The media industry, once considered immune to such occupational hazards, is now grappling with its own asbestos crisis. In February 2025, reports surfaced that at least four former ABC employees—technical staff and a broadcaster—had died from mesothelioma after exposure at the public broadcaster's former Melbourne studios in Elsternwick, operational until 2017, and Broadcast House in the CBD, home to ABC radio until the late 1980s.

These facilities were contaminated with asbestos, shedding hazardous fibres that endangered workers over the decades. The ABC now faces a wave of compensation claims from former staff, a grim echo of Trevor Grant's experience at *The Age* and *The Herald*.

The media's asbestos problem may extend beyond Melbourne. A disturbing cancer cluster at the ABC's Brisbane studios, where 10 women were diagnosed with invasive breast cancer between 1994 and 2006, raised alarms. This represented a sixfold increase in risk compared to the general female population of Queensland.

While asbestos was not definitively linked to these cases, it was never ruled out, and recent studies suggest asbestos exposure may elevate breast cancer risk, particularly in postmenopausal women. These revelations underscore the pervasive and unpredictable nature of asbestos-related diseases, which continue to claim lives in ways that defy expectation.

The dangers of asbestos also extend to workers on reality TV shows like *The Block* and *The Renovators*. DIY home renovators have long been warned about exposure to asbestos-containing materials like fibro sheeting, water pipes, flue pipes, and insulation.

The Asbestos Diseases Society of Australia, a vital resource for victims and their families, emphasises that while early detection of mesothelioma has improved, there remains no definitive treatment or cure. Patients are left with limited options as the disease progresses.

This tribute to Trevor Grant is a reminder of the fragility of life, the power of one voice to make a difference, and the importance of standing up for truth, even in the face of overwhelming odds. His legacy

Chapter 10 A Lethal Legacy

lives on in the fight for justice, in the stories of those who refuse to be silenced, and in the hope that future generations will be spared the pain of this tragedy.

For those seeking further information or support, the Asbestos Diseases Society of Australia offers resources, advocacy, and a lifeline for victims and their families. Trevor's voice, like the dust of Wittenoom, lingers—a warning, a plea, and a call to ensure that there is support for those affected by the silent killer that is asbestos.

Thanks to the Asbestos Diseases Society of Australia. The Australian Institute of Health and Welfare Agency. Asbestos and Silica Safety and Eradication Agency. The ABC, Maurice Blackburn, Slater and Gordon.

CHAPTER 11

Tunnels to Our Past

There was an unwritten rule in television – no pictures, no story. As this story nearly ended in tragedy, all we are left with are words.

It was December 1988, when I found myself standing on the banks of Melbourne's Yarra River, watching two young men prepare for a journey into the unknown.

Chapter 11 Tunnels to Our Past

They began climbing down the steep bank and wading along the shallow waters of the Yarra. The entrance to a drain ahead of them was almost hidden in a secluded culvert, its dark mouth barely visible beneath the overgrown reeds. From my position, the dark hole represented a sinister portal into our past and I felt a mix of excitement and unease. This was their world, not mine, and was steeped in history and the unknown.

As they approached the opening, I felt they were more concerned about breaching their code of secrecy by contacting the media than being caught by the law. There was a final furtive check around to see if anyone was looking. My response was the same, but by the time I turned back, they had disappeared. And that would be the last time I ever saw them.

* * *

The story began a week earlier with a phone call from two young members of a group called the 'Cave Clan'. They consisted of similar-minded urban explorers who lived to explore Melbourne's underground tunnel system. "Would you be interested in doing a story on us?" they asked. Intrigued by the idea, I agreed but explained that I needed some background information before committing a camera crew to an area that posed certain risks and suggested a dry run first as proof it could succeed.

As I delved deeper into their world, I learned that the Cave Clan was a loosely organized group of adventurers who sought out hidden and forgotten spaces beneath the city. Their explorations took them through stormwater drains, abandoned subway tunnels, and other subterranean passages that most people never even knew existed. For them, it wasn't just about the thrill of discovery; it was also about documenting and preserving the history of these underground labyrinths.

Just as arteries and veins ebb and flow beneath the surface of the human body, so too does a similar network which sustains the heart of a city.

An underground network of pipes delivers life-sustaining water through one system, while a series of drains expel our human waste through the other.

If ever this system fails, then the effects can be terminal for both; as it very nearly was for the city of Melbourne in the 1800's.

Had it not been for a system of tunnels and drains that began to be dug in 1870, Melbourne would

Chapter 11 Tunnels to Our Past

have undoubtedly drowned in the slime of human excrement or died from multiple diseases such as typhoid, diphtheria, tuberculosis, measles and scarlet fever that flowed down city gutters.

Today the old drains continue to exist. Hidden streams continue to flow and while new tunnels are being dug, old ones are being rediscovered.

The drains still pose dangers but only to the brave and foolish who risk their lives and the laws to crawl and wade their way through this underground labyrinth, tracing a course back through these 'portals into our past'.

It was agreed I would meet them as they emerged from a re-entry point not far from the Prahran railway station near a culvert that ran alongside a local sporting field. This was the original source of what was once called the 'Dismal Swamp'.

What made this swamp so dismal in the 1800s was the human excrement and animal waste continually being dumped into this cesspool of fermenting filth.

Initially, it was a natural swamp fed by a tributary or creek named 'Hawk's Burn' which ran from the nearby Malvern Hills, just east of Melbourne.

But when it rained the fetid wash with its familiar

stench began to overflow and the *'Dismal Swamp'* also became known as *'Valley of Death'* and *'Slough of Despond'*.

Down it flowed, churning and spewing its detritus contents through the cheap low-floored worker's cottages in Prahran and on into the Yarra – until the underground drain was built.

I discovered more information about the Cave Clan through a freelance writer named Daron Richter, who had been documenting their exploits. The group had been formed on Anzac Day in 1986 by three teenagers with a passion for exploring Melbourne's forgotten drains. Over time, their ranks had grown, and they had become the largest urban exploration group in Australia. But they were also fiercely secretive, operating under a strict code of anonymity.

When two members of the clan—known only as "Macca" and "Rocky"— first approached me about a potential TV news story, I was intrigued. They were in their late teens, full of youthful bravado, and eager to share their experiences. But there were caveats to our agreement. They insisted on maintaining their anonymity, and they warned me that entering the drains was illegal, punishable by a $20,000 fine.

I agreed we would be interested in doing a story

provided they would perform a "dry run" first to plan the logistics and eliminate any risks posed to a camera crew.

I was able to trace their route to some extent from a rudimentary map they had drawn from the experience of others.

I had been made aware of their first sensory reaction on entering the wide red-brick passage. They would be confronted by a musty smell, and the sound; almost silent, except for a scurrying rat, an occasional cricket or cockroach escaping the dripping water which trickled down a central culvert.

The trickle would blend into a dull rumble from constant traffic passing overhead. And as their light faded they would be forced to switch on the beams of their torches, highlighting the walls covered in graffiti.

There were many unknown extensions ahead of them, which led off beneath the city and the suburban grid. Some tunnels were dry while others carried remnants of original streams which still flowed occasionally.

The end of some extensions were marked on their map as *'manhole covers'* opening onto a suburban street or local football field to be used as possible escapes in the event of a quick exit. Not likely on this trip as the bureau had forecast fine warm weather. The rule of their unwritten law was *'Rain, then no drain'*.

The drain they planned to explore first was known as the 'Maze Drain'—a sprawling network of tunnels and maintenance shafts that stretched for kilometres beneath the city. According to Macca and Rocky, it was one of the most challenging sections of Melbourne's underground system, with countless offshoots and dead ends. Navigating it required skill, patience, and a good map.

From the map I had been given, I could see that the explorers would face a series of challenges as they made their way through the drain. They would climb down metal ladders, squeeze through rusty grates, and wade past rank, reeking waterfalls. At one point, they would encounter a pair of massive steel pipes, where twin streams of water converged into an underground inlet of the river. Beyond that, they would enter a corrugated tunnel that snaked toward a glimmer of light—a reminder of the world above.

The first chamber was described as 'large and familiar' as it represented a meeting place of the 'Cave Clan' members, similar to the nearby *'Anzac Drain'* so named because the clan discovered it on Anzac Day in 1986 and used it primarily for initiation ceremonies

Chapter 11 Tunnels to Our Past

for new members.

Another daunting section of their journey was yet to come. Near the end of the drain, they would reach a nondescript culvert that descended into another system known as the G.O.D Drain. This section was marked by a deep drop, where a dirty stream of water cascaded down a slippery stairway. To reach the next level, they would be forced to climb a warped metal ladder, its rungs twisted and its limbs buckled. It was a perilous climb, but one they had done before.

Their descriptions largely matched those of other similar-minded urban explorers who had preceded their journey.

Resting at the top they had planned to use their time to catch their breath and snack on their prepacked Mars bars. However, given my knowledge of the disease and filth that once flowed before them, eating or drinking anything in that environment would have been my last choice.

As I traced their path on the map, I couldn't help but feel a sense of dread. The final leg of their journey would take them through a section called "The Shrinker", where the wide tunnel narrowed into a square passage. This was where claustrophobia often struck as explorers were forced to crawl on their hands and knees through the cramped space. The air was putrid, with only the occasional relief from passing drains. It was a test of endurance, both physical and mental. Other clan members likened their experiences to *'crawling on knees, sucking up fresh air like an addict before detox'*

Several hours after leaving them on the banks of the Yarra I estimated they would soon be approaching the final leg of their trek leading to our planned meeting place.

But as I waited for them at the rendezvous point, I couldn't shake the feeling that something had gone wrong. They never emerged.

Hours passed, and there was no sign of the explorers so I returned to the office. Had they gotten lost? Were they injured?

Just as I was about to notify the police, I received a call from the Alfred Hospital. Macca and Rocky were safe, but they had emerged from the drain bloodied, bruised, and shaken. Their injuries were minor, but the mental impact of their ordeal would take time to heal.

It was shortly after their journey through the Shrinker that they had taken a terrifying turn. At first, they had noticed cobwebs catching in their hair as they crawled

Chapter 11 Tunnels to Our Past

through the dry, dusty pipes. But as they pressed on, the webs grew thicker, and the air grew heavier.

In the fading light of their torches, they saw movement on the walls around them—dozens of spiders, their round black bodies marked by bright red stripes.

Panic set in as the spiders began to descend, their webs spiralling down into the cramped space. Macca and Rocky were bitten multiple times, their hands and legs throbbing with pain. They knew the spiders were redbacks—venomous, but not necessarily fatal. Still, the experience was harrowing. They crawled forward on bleeding hands and knees, shouting and waving their arms to fend off the creatures. Finally, they reached a glimmer of light and emerged into the open air, where they hailed a cab to the hospital.

Macca and Rocky recovered from their ordeal but vowed never to return to the drains. For me, the experience was a reminder of the dangers that lurk in the hidden corners of our world.

I couldn't help but think about their courage, their curiosity, and their unwavering sense of adventure. They had explored a side of Melbourne that few will ever see. But I also know that some places are best left unexplored, their secrets buried in the darkness where they belong.

Epilogue

They did recover from their ordeal, but vowed never to return, and I never pursued it.

What started as three Melbourne teenagers sneaking into drains soon became the largest consolidated group of urban explorers with chapters in all capital cities around Australia. Perhaps they do it for altruistic purposes but their stories have become more of a tribute to the engineering skills of those who built our underground systems to save the greater systems above.

And as Melbourne boasts one of the largest tunnel systems in the world, said to extend over 15 hundred kilometres, there is much to be discovered.

I am reminded of that unwritten rule in television – 'no pictures, no story'.

As this story nearly ended in tragedy, at least their words painted a picture.

My thanks to 'Macca' and 'Rocky' and their fellow urban explorers. To Daron Richter a freelance writer and photographer, and to other members of the 'Cave Clan' who wish to retain their anonymity.

CHAPTER 12

A Personal Curtain Call.

'I took my cue from the voice that responded to my knock on his office door and so began a personal history of Australian Theatre from its legends Sir Frank Tait and John MacCallum'.

If anyone ever learns from the stories of others, how lucky was I to discover the history of Australian Theatre from the very legends themselves.

Melbourne's Her Majesty's Theatre (affectionately known as Her Maj) not only stands as a true icon of Australian theatre but continues to uphold the tradition she established when her curtain rose for the first time on 19 May 1867. Behind her curtain, the real-life dramas almost paled against the dramas that unfolded on her stage. As a 16-year-old in my first job on leaving school, I became part of the company they proudly called 'The Firm'.

January 1959

I took my cue from the voice that responded to my knock on his office door and entered the room. The man behind the voice (and the partly opened door) sounded neither as commanding nor theatrical as I had expected. His reputation was held in the highest regard as a businessman with an unbending passion for his work, he 'lived for his work'. And yes I was intimidated.

He was the last survivor of five brothers from Australia's greatest theatrical dynasty and now, Sir Frank Tait, who sat behind a huge mahogany desk in an equally oversized office on the third floor of Melbourne's Comedy Theatre, had just become my first boss.

Chapter 12 A Personal Curtain Call.

I was introduced as the new office boy whose duties would include handling his mail, licking his stamps and banking the previous night's takings from Her Majesty's and the Comedy Theatre in Melbourne's Exhibition Street.

My Fair Lady was performing brilliantly at Her Majesty's, while *The Odd Couple* was about to end its run at the Comedy Theatre directly beneath us. At 16 years of age, it was the perfect job to see me through the next 18 months while I was training as a radio announcer – although I never told him that.

"Welcome to 'The Firm'," he said.

From that moment on, I had a front-row seat into the final years of the world's greatest theatrical empire, which had begun to form back in 1874.

The first theatre to be established in Melbourne was a run-down timber pub on Bourke Street called 'Eagle Tavern'. From the days of settlement, as Melbourne's population began to grow so too did their desire to be entertained. The number of theatres grew exponentially with the influx of new arrivals including The Royal Victoria, otherwise known as the Pavilion, the Theatre Royal and the Victoria Saloon. All were producing a series of amateur performances led by professional actor George Buckingham.

In 1845, a more substantial venue of bricks and stone known as Queens Theatre Royal opened, adopting the name of its location in Queens Street. With the gold rush and an influx of new settlers the demand for entertainment increased further and larger venues were built, some holding up to 3,000 people.

Entertainment then began to shift from the western end of the city to the top end of Bourke Street, Lonsdale Street and Spring Street. This was the foundation for today's Melbourne theatre precinct where international stars such as actor GV Brooke, singers such as Catherine Hayes and Anna Bishop and the notorious Lola Montez were guaranteed to draw sell-out crowds.

Australia's first large-scale opera company was formed by WS Lyster in 1861 and toured the Australian colonies until he died in 1880. Live theatre soon began appealing to an even wider audience with moneyed classes paying up to seven shillings to sit in the dress circle, while the so-called 'lower orders' paid up to one shilling for 'the pits'. Christmas pantomimes also became popular with children and adults, particularly the perennial favourites: *Jack and the Beanstalk* and *Cinderella*.

Theatre in Melbourne quickly evolved, but in a

rather *ad hoc* fashion, without the influence of what we call today 'the entrepreneur'. That all changed in 1880 with the arrival of an American actor, James Cassius Williamson and his wife, actress Maggie Moore.

James Cassius Williamson

Williamson and wife Maggie struck gold with their comedy production *Struck Oil*. What was meant to be a 12-week tour of Australia by this American entrepreneur, ended up lasting for fifteen months netting Williamson £15,000, which he used to launch his career as a theatre manager in Melbourne.

He began by forming his (Royal) Comic Opera Company and in 1881 became the sole lessee of Melbourne's Theatre Royal, introducing enormous technical facilities and lavish sets. From the 1890s to 1910 (early days of cinema) audiences were still being thrilled by the realism of the stage. Intricate machinery was being applied involving live horses and moving sets, including water tanks, which added reality to scenes of a heroine being rescued from drowning.

In December 1886, Williamson opened the newly built Melbourne's Princess Theatre in Spring Street but nine years later decided to move his business operations around the corner to the Alexandra Theatre in Exhibition Street.

After minor refurbishment, the Alexandra was renamed Her Majesty's Theatre, after Queen Victoria, and re-opened on 19 May 1900.

World War 1 made it difficult for overseas artists to travel, forcing Melbourne to rely on local talent to stage patriotic fundraisers. Lavish musicals soon followed including Geelong-born Oscar Asch's *Chu Chin Chow* and *Maid of the Mountains* which made a star of Gladys Moncrieff.

Prima ballerina Anna Pavlova, danced in the mid to late 20s and Dame Nellie Melba followed the success of her 1908 grand opera tour.

While Williamson's theatrical life may have been booming, his personal life was becoming a shamble. Wife, Maggie Moore, left him for actor Harry Roberts, then she made financial claims against him, which he defended in court claiming he would "rather go to jail than pay for her debts". Maggie successfully appealed and they were eventually divorced in 1899 on the grounds of adultery.

Thirteen years later, James Cassius Williamson died leaving behind a strong theatrical empire that became

Chapter 12 A Personal Curtain Call.

the largest theatrical firm in the world. It was into this organisation that the Melbourne Tait brothers would merge their theatrical interests.

Tait Bothers

Charles Tait, the eldest of five brothers and the producer of the world's first feature movie, *The Story of the Kelly Gang*, had already established himself as theatrical entrepreneur.

In 1902, his three other brothers – John, Nevin and Frank – joined forces with Charles to form a promotional company for a series of live concerts based at Melbourne's Athenaeum Hall in Collins Street. Their concerts often included popular, short, film screenings which led them to the joint production of *The Story of the Kelly Gang* which premièred on Boxing Day 1906.

In 1920 two of the Tait brothers merged their interests with JC Williamson Ltd renaming their theatre His Majesty's following the death of Queen Victoria.

In 1924, the brothers were alerted to the imminent arrival of radio. Under the banner of JC Williamson Ltd, they were granted the licence for radio station 3LO in Melbourne. When 3LO came under the control of the government-franchised Australian Broadcasting Co., they then successfully bid for the licence to operate 3AW where they began broadcasting from original studios in His Majesty's Theatre.

In 1920, JC Williamson built the Comedy Theatre on the site once occupied by George Coppins' Olympic. After a shaky start, the Comedy became the preferred venue for modern drama and light comedies. Nine years after the Comedy was built, a fire broke out in His Majesty's Theatre destroying the auditorium and its foyer. It was a precursor of the Great Depression, which then struck all forms of life in Melbourne.

In 1934, with its auditorium and foyer rebuilt, His Majesty's reopened with the spectacular performance of *White Horse Inn*. Towards the end of 1933 Francis W Thring (Frank's dad) presented the Australian musical *Collit's Inn* at the Princess Theatre triggering a host of other musicals to follow. Repertory Theatres also began to abound providing entertainment in the suburbs, as they do today.

During World War II former Pavlova dancer Edouard Boravansky founded his ballet company under the aegis of JC Williamson, who also presented a seemingly endless stream of drawing-room comedies and revivals of Gilbert and Sullivan operettas. Local favourites

Chapter 12 A Personal Curtain Call.

included Rene 'Mo', George Wallace, Jim Gerald and Jenny Howard.

After the war, The Tivoli reverted to imported acts, namely British stars such as Tommy Trinder, Arthur Askey and George Formby. The Princess then resumed its role as a live theatre, becoming the base for entrepreneur Garnet H Carroll. However, the introduction of television in 1956 began to erode live theatre audiences and the Garnet H Carroll organisation did not survive after he died in 1964.

From 1928, the Tait's took full control of 'The Firm' from their offices in the Comedy Theatre directly opposite The Maj on Exhibition Street. Following the subsequent deaths of all his brothers, Frank Tait emerged as joint Managing Director with actor John McCallum.

John McCallum

As office boy to both men, I warmed to McCallum far more than Sir Frank, an association I would renew more than 35 years later when McCallum arrived at Network Ten as a guest on Bert Newton's GMA show.

Sir Frank may have held the top position but in my mind, McCallum waved the company flag. His high profile with JCW came after years of enhancing the golden era of British cinema, co-starring in multiple films with his adoring wife Googie Withers. Like James Cassius Williamson before him, he was married to a high-profile actress. Unlike his predecessor, McCallum's marriage lasted.

McCallum's office in the Comedy Theatre was linked to Sir Frank's by an interconnecting door but whenever I attended, that door was always shut. They had little in common. McCallum did however, speak fondly of his years with The Firm and most respectfully of Sir Frank Tait.

According to John, "Frank was tough, even ruthless in money matters, but generous in other ways... It could not have been easy for him, at the age of 75, to take control of the business that he and his brothers had built up over 40 years."

When McCallum was made joint Managing Director, it was intended that Frank would gradually retire. But the theatre business was 'meat and drink' to him. He could not give it up. Apart from his work and his family, he had no other interests, and no hobbies. According to McCallum, "He never took holidays, only a few days at Christmas and New Year, when he went down to his seaside home at Sorrento."

Chapter 12 A Personal Curtain Call.

McCallum recalled the day Frank Tait was knighted in 1956, at the age of 72. The story goes that when the news came through Tait was heard to mutter, "A knighthood? But I'd rather have the rights to *My Fair Lady*."

In the end, of course, he got both. It was his dream to present Joan Sutherland in her homeland and he did finally fulfil that dream too. Shortly after the end of her triumphant season, I found myself announcing the death of Sir Frank Tait while reading television news on TNT9 in Tasmania.

With the passing of Sir Frank, I then watched with more than just a passing interest as conflict arose within the JC Williamson organisation between John McCallum, the Managing Director and John McFarlane, Managing Director of the parent company, JC Williamson Ltd.

In 1969 both men resigned and The Firm formed a partnership with the Herald and Weekly Times of Melbourne. The Tivoli ceased production in 1966 and was destroyed by fire the following year.

In 1990, The Princess reopened after extensive refurbishment by its new owner David Marriner who left just one seat vacant on that opening night for its resident ghost, Frederick Federici.

Frederick Federici was a British actor who had migrated to Melbourne and played many roles in Gilbert and Sullivan operas with the JC Williamson Company. On the opening night of Gounod's opera *Faust* in 1888, after singing his final note as Mephistopheles, Federici descended through a trap door in the stage and suffered a fatal heart attack. Ever since then, legend holds that his ghost still haunts the Princess Theatre. A legend upheld by the likes of Bert Newton, Marina Prior and Lisa McCune who claim to have encountered his spirit many times over the years.

True or otherwise, management maintained the tradition of saving him a seat for every opening night performance – just in case. After the refurbishment of the Princess, David Marriner also restored the Regent and the Forum in Flinders Street and then bought the Comedy Theatre, where my brief life with The Firm had its beginnings in 1959.

In 1971, Williamson-Edgley Theatres was set up as a subsidiary of JC Williamson Theatres Ltd, with Michael Edgley as Managing Director. Edgley withdrew a year later.

Today the Maj is owned by another former colleague, entrepreneur, Mike Walsh, who maintained the proud

Chapter 12 A Personal Curtain Call.

theatrical tradition and helped shape a theatre precinct – arguably one of the finest in any capital cities of the world. As I was frequently told *'Movies will make you famous, Television will make you rich, but theatre will make you good'*.

(Adapted from memories, The State Library, Mimi Colligan and Frank Van Stratten)

CHAPTER 14

Load of Old Crocs

The growth of crocodiles in suburban Melbourne highlights the potential dangers of keeping exotic animals in urban settings and the risks they pose to both the animals and the community.

Beneath the veneer of normalcy throughout Melbourne's suburban life there exists fascinating stories where boundaries blur between human compassion and wildlife conservation.

Chapter 14 Load of Old Crocs

These are stories of living alongside creatures that belong far away from human habitation, yet many are convinced these wild ones can be domesticated with love and affection.

* * *

The house was an outstanding example of circa-1890, superbly renovated, surrounded by a low white picket fence and tall greenery concealing a beautifully manicured front garden. Positioned on a corner block in Melbourne's leafy suburb of Camberwell, it was obvious that whoever owned the house took much pride in maintaining its tradition. What was not traditional was lurking in the lower basement.

Based on nothing more than hearsay from a local tradesman who had been called to investigate the cause of an electrical fault, and if his claims were true, then it was the story, not the electrical fault, that was worth investigating.

His call to the newsroom simply stated he had been nearly attacked by a crocodile. Furthermore, he said the basement was full of snakes.

He refused to join us, fearing he would lose his job

for breaching company privacy laws, but his reticence was not shared by the chief of staff or the cameraman. So off we went.

Bracing for a full onslaught of accusations of intrusion, I knocked on the front door. It was opened by a middle-aged woman with a full head of grey wispy hair, supporting a first impression of an alternative lifestyle.

I introduced myself as a reporter for Channel Ten News. She immediately responded, 'My name is Silvia, and I know why you're here. It's the crocodile, isn't it?', 'Well yes', I replied, 'could we talk to you about it?'. 'Of course, do you want to talk about the snakes too'?

Slowly, her story unfolded.

From a very early age, her son Graham, who had been diagnosed on the spectrum of some disorder had developed allergic reactions to any animal with fur.

'But we discovered he was attracted to cold-blooded reptiles, so she and her husband (since deceased) bought him a tiny freshwater crocodile.

'When you feed these creatures, she said, 'of course they grow. ' Then, it was felt the croc needed a companion'.

'By the time my son was a teenager, the basement had been equipped with automatic water reticulation and

Chapter 14 Load of Old Crocs

appropriate temperature controls. The snakes were housed in special glass houses and fed live mice'.

I then informed her I would need to approach a spokesperson from Fisheries and Wildlife to obtain a comment, which I eventually did, and they removed the reptiles to an appropriate sanctuary in Ballarat.

I discovered several years later that her son had since become one of Australia's foremost experts on crocodiles and certain reptiles and was often called upon for professional advice.

And it seems he was called upon quite frequently.

* * *

Two decades later, a similar story emerged at Rockbank East of Melbourne.

Vicki Lowings, a self-confessed 'wildlife educator' had shared her humble home with an unusual family: five crocodiles. Three of these reptiles moved with her from New South Wales about ten years earlier, and her "float" – a term used for a group of crocs – had since grown to include two baby crocodiles.

Her unconventional family captured widespread attention when a short video documentary about her lifestyle went viral, amassing over two million views online.

Her crocodiles included Jilfia, or "Jilly," a 12-year-old saltwater croc measuring 2.6 meters long. Jilly happened to reside in a bungalow at the back of her property. Indoors, she shared her home with two freshwater crocs – Johnie, a 22-year-old female, and Fovian, an 11-year-old male – along with their two offspring, JJ and FJ, named after their parents.

Vicky had been living with the reptiles for more than 30 years and, by now, had accepted public criticism.

"I've been called crazy all my life, but that's all right," she says.

"They're a terrific pet. I mean, they're wildlife and you've got to respect that, and so long as you give them what they would get in the wild, you can still have them as a pet as well."

'Johnny, for example, answers to her name, (Johnny I assumed was bi-sexual) who occasionally slept in Vicky's bed and even accompanied her on walks through the neighbourhood.

"I put a harness on her and taught her with a lead so she could just walk alongside me."

However, not all her neighbours shared her love of

Crocs and some complained to the authorities.

Devoting much of her life to caring for her unique pets she sparked such curiosity in the community that locals even helped raise nearly $3,000 through an online crowdfunding campaign to build a proper enclosure in her backyard.

Her goal was to challenge misconceptions about crocodiles. "People say they only eat rotten meat – that's not true," she explained. "They're very sensitive, intelligent animals with emotions. They're often misunderstood because they're portrayed as instinctive killers. Like any wild animal, they kill to eat, but there's another side to them that I've seen. With the right stimulation, they're entirely different creatures."

Her crocodiles were fed a diet of whole fish, chicken, rats, and mice. "They don't like feathers or fur, so Jilly sometimes gets chicken wings, which I supplement with vitamins and minerals."

Despite her deep love for crocodiles, Vicki Lowings cautions others against keeping them as pets. "More people in Victoria are starting to keep crocodiles, which I don't support," she said. "They're specialist animals. I have all the necessary permits and licenses, but they're not for everyone. People think I'm crazy for having a saltwater crocodile, and that's when authorities stepped in.

Her dedication to her crocodiles was not shared by all.

As Vicki argued, they weren't just 'pets' she had a licence to take them around to schools and community centres to raise awareness that not all crocs eat you. But authorities decided to suspend her licence and take away her pet crocodiles.

Jilly was transported to the Northern Territory to be introduced to other Crocs, but Vicki worried about how she would cope without her. "They bond with their owners and they will fret, and they can die."

They are also wonderful protectors. "I'm one of the only homes in Rockbank that hasn't been broken into," she jokes.

If indeed love is in the eyes of the beholder, then these strange affairs are far more common than first thought.

* * *

The discovery of crocodiles in suburban parks and streets suggests that these stories are not isolated incidents. In 2017, a one-meter-long saltwater crocodile was found wandering the streets of Heidelberg Heights on Christmas Day. Police initially dismissed the report as a prank but were soon confronted by the reality of a crocodile on the loose. Melbourne snake catcher Mark Pelley, who was called to the scene, described the encounter as one of the most surreal moments of his career.

"I found five police members being stared down by a decent-sized crocodile, and the crocodile wouldn't back down."

Similarly, in 2024, a dead freshwater crocodile was discovered in Ruffey Lake Park in Doncaster. Wildlife photographer Andrew Wallis, who stumbled upon the carcass, speculated that the animal had been kept as a pet before being released into the wild. "It's possible whoever had the crocodile thought it was looking a bit under the weather and would be far better off if returned to the wild," he said.

These incidents highlight the risks of keeping exotic pets in suburban settings. While some owners, like Silvia and Vicki, are deeply committed to the welfare of their animals, others may lack the knowledge or resources to care for them properly. The release of crocodiles into the wild not only endangers the animals but also poses a threat to the community.

If beauty does lie in the eye of the beholder, then the love of crocodiles is not just isolated affaires .

* * *

In June 2024, hundreds of reptiles, including crocodiles and an inland taipan, the world's deadliest snake, were evacuated after a fire broke out at a factory in Melbourne's east, killing some of the animals inside .

The Country Fire Authority responded to the fire at the Jurassic Jungle warehouse on Canterbury Road in Kilsyth to find the factory's roof fully ablaze.

Wildlife Victoria and Ambulance Victoria also attended the scene as more than 500 reptiles, many of them venomous, were kept inside the building. The factory served as a warehouse for the Jurassic Jungle store in Bayswater, which sold native and foreign animals.

Firefighters contained the fire within an hour before the building's owners and wildlife carers could remove the animals. It is believed some reptiles were killed in the blaze. Of those which survived approximately 30 animals were transported to Reptiles Victoria's rehabilitation centre where Wildlife Victoria's travelling veterinary services assisted to provide veterinary assistance.

The incident underscored the challenges of managing large collections of exotic animals.

While facilities like Jurassic Jungle play a role in wildlife education and conservation, they also carry significant risks. The fire served as a stark reminder of the need for proper safety measures and emergency preparedness.

* * *

The stories of crocodiles in suburban Melbourne reveal the complexities of human-animal relationships. For individuals like Graham and Vicki, these creatures are more than just pets; they are sources of comfort, passion, and purpose. Yet, the challenges of keeping exotic animals in urban environments cannot be ignored. From legal and ethical considerations to the risks posed to both animals and the public, these stories highlight the need for a balanced approach to wildlife conservation and exotic pet ownership. Whether it's a crocodile in a basement, a snake in a glass enclosure, or a saltwater croc wandering the streets, these stories challenge our perceptions of the natural world and our place within it. They are a testament to the enduring allure of the wild, even in the most unexpected places.

CHAPTER 15

White Light

"Near Death Experiences"

Kerry Packer, the Australian media tycoon, was a man who commanded attention. Known for his larger-than-life personality, blunt demeanour and an air of intimidation, he was a force to be reckoned with. As the head of the Nine Network and the publishing giant Australian Consolidated Press, Packer dominated the media landscape. But his influence extended beyond business; he revolutionised sports, most notably with the creation of World Series Cricket in the 1970s.

Yet, for all his achievements, it was a single moment in 1990 that helped create the image of Packer's immortality.

It was during the Australian Open polo championships in Sydney when Packer suffered a massive heart attack. Collapsing on the field, he was declared clinically dead for six minutes before being revived by ambulance officers. After fully recovering, he was characteristically blunt to a journalist when he replied, "Son, I've been to the other side, and let me tell you, there's nothing fucking there."

Packer's words were as brash as the man himself. But while his dismissal of an afterlife may resonate with some, it clashes with the profound and often life-changing accounts shared by many others around the world.

Arguably, the most documented case of NDA (near-death experience) is told by former US Marine and American businessman Dannion Brinkley.

He is a man who defied death not once, not twice, but three times.

The fact that his story has been so well documented may have something to do with the number of books he

Chapter 15 White Light

has written on his experience, but as we are exploring this subject, his stories cannot be ignored.

In 1975 while talking on the phone during a thunderstorm storm he was struck by a bolt of lightning, sending at least 180,000 volts through his body so powerful it welded his shoes to the floor. Declared clinically dead by paramedics, he woke up in the local morgue.

Over ten years later, he faced mortality once again during open heart surgery. Miraculously, Dannion Brinkly defied the odds after being declared deceased for more than 20 minutes before waking up in ICU.

A third NDA took place after brain surgery and a massive stroke, but is happy to take on the doubters and sceptics about what happens when we die.

Brinkley has since put his words into action. For decades, he's been counselling terminally ill patients, specifically fellow war veterans. He has spent countless hours reassuring those struggling with life issues and has developed an extraordinary ability to predict future events, which no one can explain.

Near-death experiences (NDE's) remain a mystery— from both a scientific and spiritual point of view, leaving us with more questions than answers.

Whether they are the final sparks of a dying brain or glimpses of something beyond, one thing is clear: they transform those who experience them in ways that defy explanation.

NDEs are not rare. Studies suggest that around 40% of people who experience cardiac arrest report some form of near-death experience. These stories transcend cultural, religious, and geographical boundaries, often sharing common themes.

Out-of-body experience:

Floating above their physical bodies, watching as medical professionals or bystanders work to save them.

Tunnels and light:

The sensation of moving through a dark tunnel toward a bright, comforting light is a recurring story.

Feelings of peace and love:

An overwhelming sense of tranquillity, unconditional love, and acceptance is frequently reported.

Encounters with entities:

Some meet deceased loved ones, spiritual beings, or a guiding presence.

Life reviews:

A vivid, panoramic replay of one's life is often accompanied by feelings of reflection or judgment.

A choice to return:

Many describe being given the option to stay in this transcendent state or return to their physical bodies.

Due to the controversial nature of the subject, many who have experienced an NDE wish to remain anonymous, but their stories, while not officially documented, often share similar elements:

Story 1.

Lara survived a severe car crash. She described feeling herself floating above the scene while watching paramedics attempting to revive her. She then described a force pulling her into a dark tunnel with a bright light at the end. She then saw shadowy figures of deceased loved ones but was told she had to return. She woke up in hospital with no medical explanation for her survival.

Story 2.

Steve suffered a heart attack and he too observed doctors trying to revive him. He was then pulled into a space where his entire life played before him, not just as memories, but as if he were reliving them. He felt not only his own emotions but also those of others he had affected, both positively and negatively. He was told it wasn't his time yet and woke up in the ICU.

Story 3.

A patient undergoing emergency surgery flatlined for several minutes. During that time, she described being greeted by her deceased grandmother and an uncle she had never met. They told her she had more to do in life. When she recovered, she recounted specific details about the uncle that she hadn't known, shocking relatives who knew him well.

Near-death experiences (NDEs) have fascinated people for centuries in the search for proof of life after death. Or is it simply the brain's last hurrah before shutting down?

From all available information, their stories appear to have common themes, with survivors often becoming more spiritual, more compassionate, and less afraid of death.

Study

Some experts believe NDEs are caused by the brain reacting to life-threatening events like heart attacks or severe injuries. These experiences likely come from changes in brain activity, not necessarily proof of an afterlife.

For example, when brain activity increases in certain areas, it can cause vivid hallucinations. High carbon dioxide levels in the blood can also create similar effects.

Other scientists believe the brain releases chemicals such as endorphins during trauma, making people feel calm and detached. The feeling of moving through a tunnel may be attributed to the brain's vision system shutting down.

Another theory raises the idea that consciousness exists outside the brain. If true, NDEs could be real glimpses of an afterlife. This is hard to prove, but some people report seeing real events while unconscious. This idea is harder to prove scientifically but is supported by cases where individuals report verifiable details from outside their physical bodies. One of the most interesting things about NDEs is how they often change people's personalities and beliefs in their future lives.

Another well documented case involved Dr. Eben Alexander, a neurosurgeon who once dismissed NDEs as hallucinations—until he had one himself. In 2008, a rare form of bacterial meningitis left him in a coma. While doctors believed his brain was too damaged to generate thoughts, he later described experiencing a loving presence guiding him. He went on to write a best-selling book on the subject of life after death, detailing his story and arguing that consciousness does exist beyond the brain.

Another well-documented case is Pam Reynolds, a woman who underwent a high-risk brain surgery in 1991. During the procedure, doctors drained her blood, stopped her heart, and lowered her body temperature to near-death levels. Despite being clinically "dead" with no brain activity, she later recounted conversations between specialists and described an incident when a surgical tool was dropped on the floor. Details were later confirmed by staff.

Chapter 15 White Light

Cassandra Scott was found floating face down in the water at Sydney's Coogee Beach on December 12, 2012. She had no pulse and was clinically dead for approximately 15 minutes before being resuscitated by a lifesaver and an emergency doctor who happened to be nearby. Cassandra recalls her experience as "like being asleep but aware I was sleeping." She witnessed her resuscitation from above, surrounded by four strangers who had saved her life.

The experience deepened Cassandra's appreciation for her life and the lives of others. "I used to take things for granted," she admits. "Now, I see every day as a gift."

Kate Cliff was 26 when her life took an unexpected turn. Crossing at pedestrian lights in Sydney, she was struck by a car and thrown into the air. As she lay on the ground, she watched the entire scene unfold from above. "I saw myself lying in the middle of the road, watching the medics working to revive me," she recalls.

Raised as an atheist, Kate had always been searching for meaning. The accident radically changed her perspective. "It was like a veil had been lifted," she says. "I realised there was so much more to life than what I could see."

Kate went on to study meditation in India and helped others find meaning and empowerment.

Alistair Blake from Victoria is one man who knows more about the topic than most having been "Technically dead for 90 minutes". The day began very normally. He rode 45 kilometres on his bike and spent time with Melinda – his wife of 35 years – before he headed off to bed. It was around 3.10 am when Melinda woke to find Alistair suffering a medical episode.

"She grabbed her mobile phone and dialled triple-0, where medics instructed her how to perform CPR. By the time they arrived, police had informed Melinda that her husband was unlikely to survive. For 90 minutes, paramedics fought to restart Alistair's heart, and just when they were about to stop, they miraculously found a pulse. Almost a week later, Alistair woke up at Frankston Hospital and remarkably, there were no signs of a brain injury. As a result, his medical team nicknamed him 'Lazarus' – the man who was raised from the dead.

"No bright lights" he said, "no out-of-body experience, nothing like that whatsoever, considering I was technically dead for 90 minutes".

Chapter 15 White Light

* * *

Near-death experiences remain a mystery—one that bridges science and spirituality, leaving us with more questions than answers. Whether they are the final sparks of a dying brain or glimpses of something beyond, one thing is clear: they transform those who experience them in ways that defy explanation.

Perhaps the real takeaway of NDE's isn't about what happens after we die—it's about how we choose to live.

Kerry Packer's blunt dismissal of an afterlife stands in contrast to the deeply held personal and often life-altering accounts of others.

However, one can also argue his own near-death experience in 1990 inspired another side to his life, helping others by donating portable defibrillators to the NSW Ambulance Service.

Perhaps Kerry Packer was right. 'Son, I've been to the other side, and let me tell you, there's nothing fucking there"

The fact is Kerry Packer may have been closer to the other side several times due to his health struggles. His heart disease and kidney ailments are well-documented, and his kidney transplant in 2000, donated by his friend Nicholas Ross, was a testament to the loyalty and friendship between the two men.

His first death took place during the Australian Open polo championships in Sydney in October 1990.

His final breath came at his home in Sydney on December 26, 2005, nine days after his 68th birthday. Knowing that his health was already failing with kidney disease, he instructed his doctors not to revive or artificially prolong his life with dialysis.

His death marked the end of an era for Australian media and business. His impact continues to be felt in the industries he shaped to this day, leaving behind a legacy of business acumen, philanthropy, and a reputation for being unapologetically himself.

As for hi final journey to the other side, we will never know.

'Saved by the Light' and 'At Peace in the Night' – Dannion Brinkly

CHAPTER 16.

My Hidden Headlines.

Throughout history, mankind has always been possessed by a thirst for knowledge.

We have always sought to know why things happen and then pushed the boundaries to discover what was possible thereafter. The power of knowledge has not only shaped our very existence but has given enormous prestige to the storytellers who have been charged with passing that knowledge down through the ages.

Most historians believe that storytelling has defined our humanity. We are the only creatures on earth who create and tell stories. Since the first cave paintings were etched more than 40,000 years ago, telling stories has been one of the most fundamental methods of recording our history. From myths to legends, fairy tales to fables, they have not only reflected the wisdom and knowledge from our past but have shaped our future.

We all possess an innate human propensity to share what we know; it is part of our human psyche. How often have we all enjoyed a certain satisfaction in passing on hitherto unknown stories or information? Or being among the first to hear those stories? Like hit songs, the bigger they are, the more we tend to remember where we were when we first heard them.

Psychologists believe people share knowledge and information because it also allows us to feel more involved and perhaps more important in the eyes of others.

According to Freud: *There is one longing–almost as deep, almost as imperious as the desire for food or sleep.*

Chapter 16. My Hidden Headlines.

That is "the desire to be great." Others have called it "the desire to be important."

I believe the driving force behind becoming a TV newsreader came from an inherent desire to inform, to seek out a story and tell it. I have always considered myself a storyteller – nothing more – so I made a career out of it like many storytellers before me from the caves to the "bardic disciples" of the Middle Ages.

The Minstrel

The lilt of his lute broke the dawn at its stillest Wretch'd and weary yet still eag'r to fillest of battles and plague from a land b'rne of tears, A king his queen their l'res and their sears And the village stood mute in rapture 'r naught As the minstrel f'rtold what his god had wrought

Today, the lute is long gone.

News was once delivered from the village square – now the global village is accessible in every home. Tales are similar: battles, wars, leaders, laws, even light-hearted trivia of modern-day seers. The reporters gather the information, but each night, when a familiar theme rolls, it's a presenter who introduces the story: presenters, anchors, newsreaders or simply "Modern Day Minstrels".

After almost seventy years of television, the most consistently watched program on nearly all networks is still the main nightly news. In that time, there has been little change to the format of our news; headlines, content, sport and the weather. In fact, it has all been very predictable.

However, behind the headlines, it was a far different story with dramatic changes continually driven by technology. I stood in awe at the introduction of satellites, welcomed the transition of black and white to colour, struggled a little with film to tape, then finally witnessed the birth of the digital computer age. I bore witness as millions of dollars were spent annually on production, research and promotion, then agonised with news editors and producers over ways to find that indefinable formula that would guarantee success for our bulletins.

Accepting the fact that television is all about perception, we continually tweaked our news in the hope that even a change in set design would attract more viewers. We experimented with pillars and posts, squares and circles, desks and chairs, untold "chroma key" backgrounds and multiple TV monitors. The only constant was the colour blue and of course, the cost. Always rising.

Chapter 16. My Hidden Headlines.

As one veteran news editor lamented when his opposition boasted a million-dollar set change, 'What's the point of redecorating a restaurant if the food is still crap?'

We attempted to change the "menu", providing an appetite for happy news, worthy news, tabloid news, overseas news, feature news, fanciful, factual and sensational news – anything to make a point of difference.

We ended up delivering a mix of all, then sat back to watch the weekly ratings to see if the viewers approved. Not exactly rocket science but almost as costly.

And as our production costs continued to rise, alternative news sources began to increase. In the last few years of my career as a newsreader, TV news viewers found these alternative sources and simply left traditional news in droves. We not only lost audience numbers but somehow lost the initiative to reinvent our ability to compete.

We were overrun by multiple digital platforms led by Facebook, Twitter and other social media outlets, and we allowed them to capture our initiative for "breaking news". Sixty years ago, breaking news was the sole domain of radio. The assassination of JFK in

1963 established a formula for live breaking news, then came the moon landing in 1969, and satellites officially stole the initiative.

As my first TV news editor John Maher, lamented in 1956 'no one complained what we did then because they knew less than we did and we knew nothing.'

Today, audiences are far more discerning. They not only watched as we stumbled into this uncharted wilderness, they even led us into it.

The first group to desert us was that vital young demographic we had all so righteously boasted as our front line of defence. They left us with a diminishing group of news consumers who were all getting older. Viewers then watched as we not only lost the initiative for breaking news but attempted to make up for that loss by using reporters to fill with superfluous waffle under the pretence it was live television. We can all point the finger of blame at others, but "beware who casts the first stone" as we were not blameless ourselves.

On the plus side as we celebrated the first 60 years of television news, we could still boast an audience reach of 85 per cent of Australian viewers. Despite those numbers having continually fallen, television news is still the most consistently watched program on most

Chapter 16. My Hidden Headlines.

networks. The question now being posed is whether TV news can continue to survive.

I fully believe it can, but I am a little unsure in what form.

I am reminded that when television first began in 1956 there was no such workplace position as "newsreader". The job evolved, as did the industry itself, and the evolution continues. I suppose in life we all hope that our contributions make some difference.

I had hoped in retirement to leave the industry in better shape than when I first started. Sadly, I am not confident my contribution had any effect at all.

If, as the doomsayers are proclaiming, this is the "beginning of the end", having seen it all from the beginning doesn't make the end any easier; it confirms that it was the journey that mattered the most.

Hidden Headlines is Mal Walden's ninth book, published by Brolga since his retirement from television in 2013.

All stories were freely told and witnessed by others to confirm authenticity. An occasional caveat was agreed to protect an identity. What ties them together is the simple yet powerful idea: everyone has a story to tell, and all it takes is someone willing to listen.

After 6 decades in the media, Mal Walden learnt to listen.

Be Published

Publish through a successful publisher.
Brolga Publishing is represented through:
- National book trade distribution, including sales, marketing & distribution through Simon & Schuster.
- International book trade distribution to:
    - The United Kingdom
    - Sales representation in South East Asia
- Worldwide e-Book distribution

For details and enquiries, contact:
Brolga Publishing Pty Ltd
ABN 46 063 962 443
PO Box 452
Torquay Victoria 3228
Australia

markzocchi@brolgapublishing.com.au
(Email for a catalogue request)